How to Use
HISTORY POCKETS

History Pockets—The American Civil War provides an exciting travel adventure back to the beginning of the United States of America. The engaging activities are stored in labeled pockets and bound into a decorative cover. Students will be proud to see their accumulated projects presented all together. At the end of the book, evaluation sheets have been added for teacher use.

Make a Pocket

1. Use a 12" x 18" (30.5 x 46 cm) sheet of construction paper for each pocket. Fold up 6" (15 cm) to make a 12" (30.5 cm) square.

2. Staple the right side of each pocket closed.

3. Punch two or three holes in the left side of each pocket.

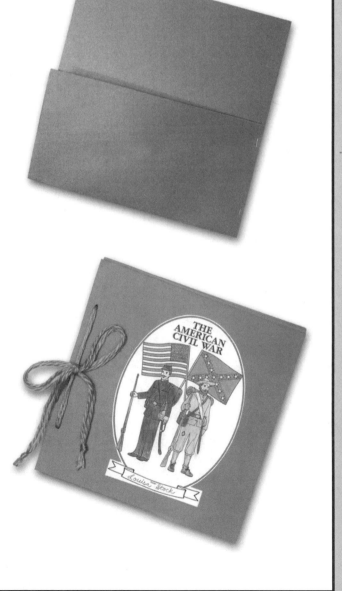

Assemble the Pocket Book

1. Reproduce the cover illustration on page 3 for each student.

2. Direct students to color and cut out the illustration and glue it onto a 12" (30.5 cm) square of construction paper to make the cover.

3. Punch two or three holes in the left side of the cover.

4. Fasten the cover and the pockets together. You might use string, ribbon, twine, raffia, or binder rings.

Every Pocket Has...

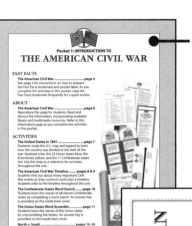

Overview Page
This teacher reference page describes the activities presented in each pocket.

Fast Facts Bookmark and Pocket Label
Reproduce the page for students. Direct students to color and cut out the pocket label and glue it onto the pocket. Cut out the bookmark and glue it onto a 4½" x 12" (11.5 x 30.5 cm) strip of construction paper.

Pocket Label

"Fast Facts" Bookmark

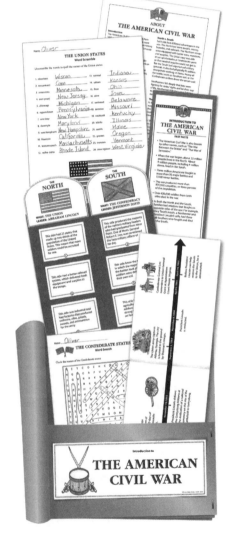

About Page
Reproduce the "About..." page. Use this information and the "Fast Facts" bookmark as references for the activities presented in the pocket.

Activities
Have students do the activities and store them in the labeled pocket.

Note: Reproduce this cover for students to color, cut out, and glue to the cover of their American Civil War book.

THE AMERICAN CIVIL WAR

Name:

Pocket 1: INTRODUCTION TO

THE AMERICAN CIVIL WAR

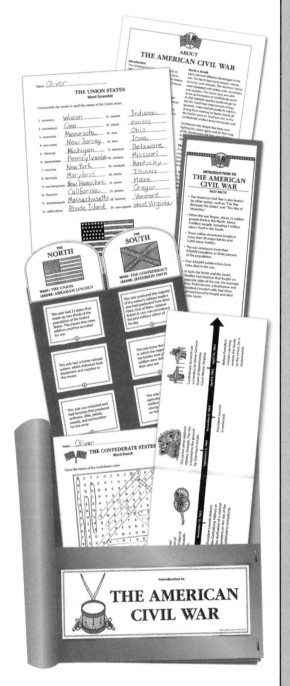

FAST FACTS

See page 2 for instructions on how to prepare the Fast Facts bookmark and pocket label. As you complete the activities in this pocket, read the Fast Facts bookmark frequently for a quick review.

ABOUT

Reproduce this page for students. Read and discuss the information, incorporating available library and multimedia resources. Refer to this information page as you complete the activities in this pocket.

ACTIVITIES

Students study the U.S. map and legend to learn how the country was divided at the start of the war. Students color the 23 Union states blue, the 8 territories yellow, and the 11 Confederate states red. Use this map as a reference for activities throughout the unit.

Students find out about many important Civil War events as they construct and color a timeline. Students refer to the timeline throughout the unit.

Students learn the names of all eleven Confederate states by completing a word search. An answer key is provided on the inside back cover.

Students learn the names of the Union states by unscrambling the letters. An answer key is provided on the inside back cover.

There were major differences between the two sides at the beginning of the Civil War. Students cut out fact cards and glue them on the correct side of an answer mat.

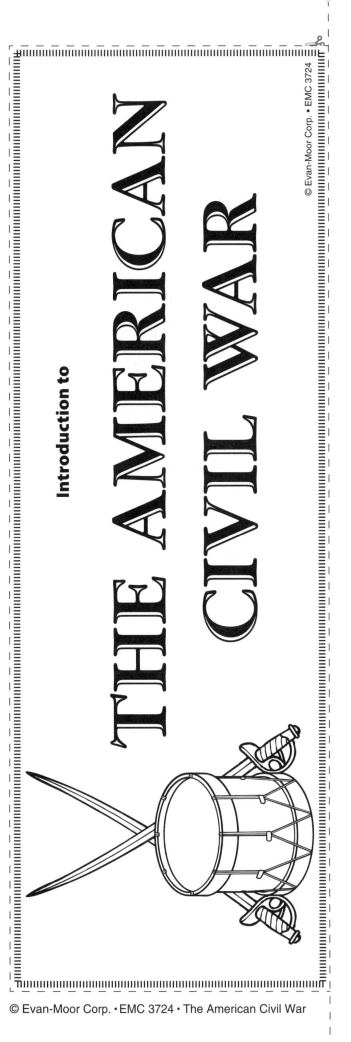

Introduction to

THE AMERICAN CIVIL WAR

INTRODUCTION TO
THE AMERICAN CIVIL WAR

FAST FACTS

- The American Civil War is also known by other names, such as "The War Between the States" and "The War of Secession."

- When the war began, about 22 million people lived in the North. About 9 million people, including 4 million slaves, lived in the South.

- Three million Americans fought in more than 50 major battles and 5,000 minor battles.

- The war produced more than 970,000 casualties, or three percent of the population.

- Over 620,000 soldiers from both sides died in the war.

- In both the North and the South, families had relatives that fought on opposite sides of the war. For example, Mary Todd Lincoln, a Northerner and President Lincoln's wife, had three half-brothers who fought and died for the South.

ABOUT
THE AMERICAN CIVIL WAR

Introduction

The American Civil War took place from 1861 to 1865. This bloody war took more American lives than any other war in history. Abraham Lincoln called the nation "a house divided."

Causes of the War

The war had many causes, but the major issue was slavery. Originally, all 13 American colonies had slavery. After the War of Independence, slavery slowly came to an end in the industrial North. But the South's economy depended on large cotton plantations worked by slaves.

In 1860, Abraham Lincoln was elected president. President Lincoln believed that slavery was wrong. An antislavery movement grew in the North. The federal government outlawed the importation of new slaves and tried to limit the use of slavery in the South. Southerners felt that their country was turning against them. One by one, Southern states seceded, or left, the Union. The eleven states formed the Confederate States of America.

The War Begins

The U.S. government, led by President Abraham Lincoln, insisted that states were not permitted to secede. This led to war. On April 12, 1861, Confederate troops fired on Fort Sumter in South Carolina, a U.S. military post. A bloody battle between the North and the South began.

North v. South

Each side had different advantages in the war. The North had more people, money, factories, and railroads. The Northern troops were equipped with better arms, munitions, and supplies. The Union navy was able to set up blockades at Confederate ports so that needed supplies could not get in. But the South had experienced military generals. It also had physically fit soldiers, strong from working on farms. Nearly all the battles were on Southern soil, so the Confederate soldiers knew the terrain well.

Southerners felt deeply that they were fighting for states' rights and for their way of life. Northerners felt they were fighting to keep the country together and to abolish slavery.

The Tide Turns

In the beginning of the war, the South won many important battles. But in 1863, the North had two important victories: Gettysburg and Vicksburg. The South never recovered.

In 1865, Confederate General Robert E. Lee surrendered to Union General Ulysses S. Grant. The Union victory eventually led to the abolition of slavery throughout the United States.

Less than a week after the war ended, Abraham Lincoln was assassinated by a Southern sympathizer.

The American Civil War • EMC 3724 • © Evan-Moor Corp.

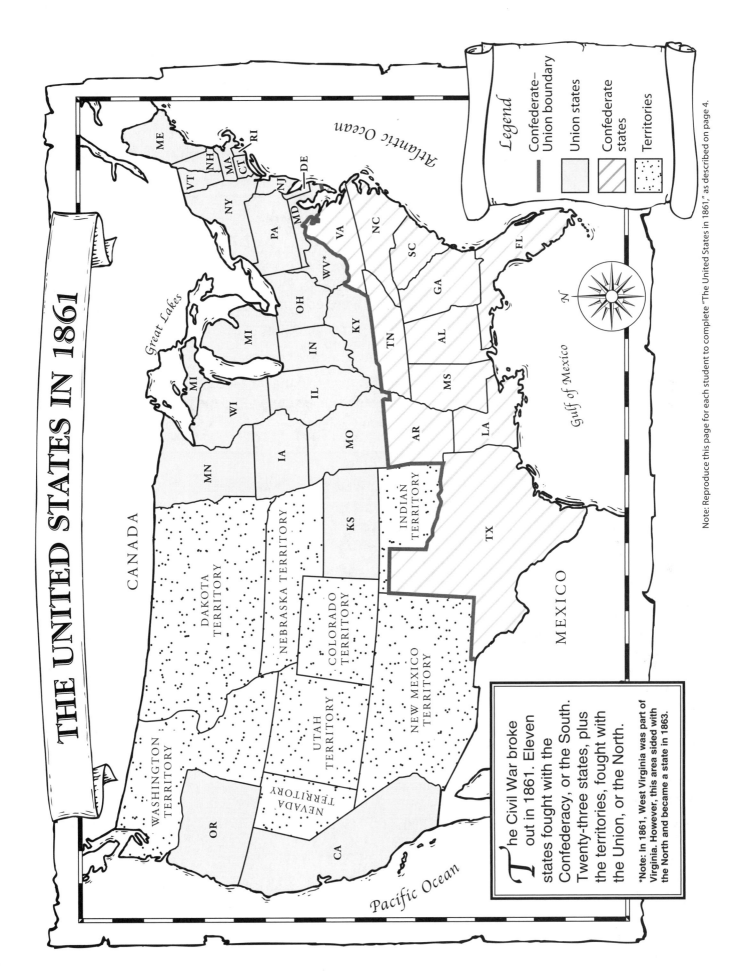

THE UNITED STATES IN 1861

Legend

— Confederate–Union boundary

☐ Union states

▨ Confederate states

⸭ Territories

Note: Reproduce this page for each student to complete "The United States in 1861," as described on page 4.

*T*he Civil War broke out in 1861. Eleven states fought with the Confederacy, or the South. Twenty-three states, plus the territories, fought with the Union, or the North.

*Note: In 1861, West Virginia was part of Virginia. However, this area sided with the North and became a state in 1863.

CANADA

Great Lakes

Atlantic Ocean

Gulf of Mexico

MEXICO

Pacific Ocean

WASHINGTON TERRITORY

OR

NEVADA TERRITORY

CA

UTAH TERRITORY

NEW MEXICO TERRITORY

DAKOTA TERRITORY

NEBRASKA TERRITORY

COLORADO TERRITORY

KS

MN

IA

MO

INDIAN TERRITORY

TX

WI

IL

IN

OH

KY

TN

AR

LA

MI

MI

NY

PA

WV*

VA

NC

SC

GA

AL

MS

FL

MD

DE

NJ

ME

VT

NH

MA

CT

RI

THE AMERICAN CIVIL WAR TIMELINE

Students assemble a timeline of important events from the Civil War. Students may refer to it periodically throughout the unit.

STEPS TO FOLLOW

1. Instruct students to cut out the timeline sections and glue or tape them together.

2. As a class, read and discuss the important dates and events of the Civil War. Note that only a sampling of the many battles and other events of the war are highlighted.

3. Have students color the pictures on the timeline.

4. Students then fold the timeline and store it in Pocket 1. Encourage students to refer to the timeline throughout the unit.

MATERIALS

- pages 8 (bottom only) and 9, reproduced for each student

- colored pencils

- scissors

- glue or transparent tape

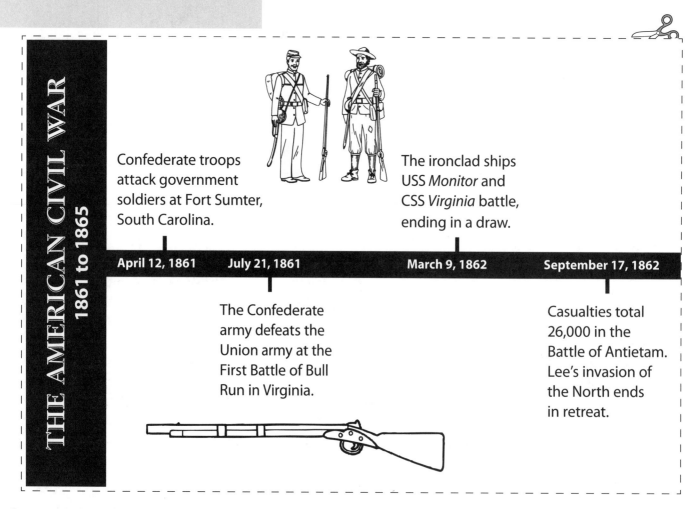

THE AMERICAN CIVIL WAR
1861 to 1865

Confederate troops attack government soldiers at Fort Sumter, South Carolina.

The ironclad ships USS *Monitor* and CSS *Virginia* battle, ending in a draw.

April 12, 1861   **July 21, 1861**   **March 9, 1862**   **September 17, 1862**

The Confederate army defeats the Union army at the First Battle of Bull Run in Virginia.

Casualties total 26,000 in the Battle of Antietam. Lee's invasion of the North ends in retreat.

President Lincoln issues the Emancipation Proclamation. This document eventually frees all slaves.

Confederate troops surrender the town of Vicksburg after 40 days of nonstop cannon assaults from Union troops.

January 1, 1863   **July 1–3, 1863**   **July 4, 1863**   **November 19, 1863**

The Union army defeats the Confederate army at the Battle of Gettysburg. This is the turning point of the war.

President Lincoln delivers the Gettysburg Address at the dedication of a national cemetery on the site of the battlefield in Gettysburg.

glue tab

The Union army captures Atlanta, Georgia. The city is burned to the ground by Sherman's troops.

Confederate General Lee surrenders to Union General Grant at Appomattox Court House, Virginia.

September 2, 1864   **November 8, 1864**   **April 9, 1865**   **April 14, 1865**

President Lincoln is reelected.

Before President Lincoln can help restore the South to the Union, he is assassinated.

glue tab

Name _____

 # THE CONFEDERATE STATES
Word Search
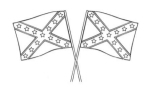

Circle the names of the Confederate states.

```
A  Z  T  C  O  C  H  C  A  A  R  A  L  A  F
N  Q  A  O  R  F  U  Y  I  M  R  H  N  J  Q
I  Q  D  R  B  K  B  G  J  K  A  I  D  V  C
L  T  I  R  K  U  R  B  A  G  L  B  I  H  F
O  E  R  H  Y  O  L  N  K  O  E  S  A  C  W
R  N  O  V  E  Q  S  O  R  Z  R  K  F  L  Q
A  N  L  G  W  A  T  A  U  T  E  X  A  S  A
C  E  F  Q  S  B  C  T  A  I  K  I  H  J  U
H  S  F  T  C  H  R  Q  N  Z  S  N  T  J  W
T  S  Q  F  T  T  M  S  O  M  M  I  O  V  O
R  E  U  U  A  I  N  I  G  R  I  V  A  D  R
O  E  O  L  G  W  L  H  I  C  T  S  H  N  V
N  S  M  I  S  S  I  S  S  I  P  P  I  B  A
P  M  V  R  I  X  U  Y  B  E  Z  V  L  I  W
J  M  K  F  V  T  X  I  X  O  Q  P  Z  Z  U
```

Alabama	Georgia	North Carolina	Texas
Arkansas	Louisiana	South Carolina	Virginia
Florida	Mississippi	Tennessee	

   The American Civil War • EMC 3724 • © Evan-Moor Corp.

THE UNION STATES
Word Scramble

Unscramble the words to spell the names of the Union states.

1. niswniocs _____

2. toncentucci _____

3. omesninta _____

4. ewn yeserj _____

5. chimnagi _____

6. nypanslivean _____

7. wne kroy _____

8. darmnyla _____

9. wen hersphami _____

10. filaarcoin _____

11. testsamssauch _____

12. redho slidna _____

13. nainaid _____

14. saksan _____

15. ihoo _____

16. aiow _____

17. earlwead _____

18. sirmoius _____

19. necktyuk _____

20. islinilo _____

21. eamin _____

22. greoon _____

23. tronmev _____

24. stew ngiaviri _____

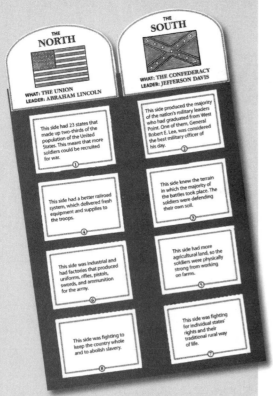

MATERIALS

- pages 13 and 14, reproduced for each student
- 9" x 12" (23 x 30.5 cm) colored construction paper
- colored pencils
- scissors
- glue

NORTH V. SOUTH

There were important differences between the Union states and the Confederate states that gave each certain advantages during the Civil War.

Students read facts and decide which side they describe. Then they glue each statement under "The North" or "The South" on an answer mat.

STEPS TO FOLLOW

1. Instruct students to fold the construction paper in half to create an answer mat.

2. Next, direct students to color and cut out the labels on page 14. Students then glue one label at the top of each side of the mat.

3. With students, reread the "North v. South" section on page 6. Students then cut out the fact cards on page 13, read each one, and decide whether it represents a fact about the North or the South. Have students place each card under the correct heading on the mat.

4. Confirm the correct answers with students. When all the cards have been correctly placed under the headings, have students glue the cards to the answer mat.

Answers:

The North: 1, 4, 6, 8

The South: 2, 3, 5, 7

FACT CARDS

This side had 23 states that made up two-thirds of the population of the United States. This meant that more soldiers could be recruited for war.

①

This side produced the majority of the nation's military leaders who had graduated from West Point. One of them, General Robert E. Lee, was considered the best military officer of his day.

②

This side knew the terrain in which the majority of the battles took place. The soldiers were defending their own soil.

③

This side had a better railroad system, which delivered fresh equipment and supplies to the troops.

④

This side had more agricultural land, so the soldiers were physically strong from working on farms.

⑤

This side was industrial and had factories that produced uniforms, rifles, pistols, swords, and ammunition for the army.

⑥

This side was fighting for individual states' rights and their traditional rural way of life.

⑦

This side was fighting to keep the country whole and to abolish slavery.

⑧

THE NORTH

WHAT: THE UNION
LEADER: ABRAHAM LINCOLN

THE SOUTH

WHAT: THE CONFEDERACY
LEADER: JEFFERSON DAVIS

THE SOUTH

WHAT: THE CONFEDERACY
LEADER: JEFFERSON DAVIS

THE NORTH

WHAT: THE UNION
LEADER: ABRAHAM LINCOLN

Pocket 2

SLAVERY IN AMERICA

FAST FACTS

See page 2 for instructions on how to prepare the Fast Facts bookmark and pocket label. As you complete the activities in this pocket, read the Fast Facts bookmark frequently for a quick review.

ABOUT

Reproduce this page for students. Read and discuss the information, incorporating available library and multimedia resources. Refer to this information page as you complete the activities in this pocket.

ACTIVITIES

After the invention of the cotton gin, the production of cotton soared. Students discuss the parts of the cotton gin and how it worked. Then they write about the importance of the cotton gin during that period of history.

Students read about the various types of people who lived and worked on a Southern plantation. Students create an accordion-fold minibook that describes the life of the planter, field slaves, house slaves, and overseer.

Students learn about John Brown, Frederick Douglass, Sojourner Truth, and Harriet Tubman as they make a pop-up book highlighting the accomplishments of these leaders of the antislavery movement.

SLAVERY IN AMERICA

SLAVERY IN AMERICA

FAST FACTS

- The words *emancipate* and *abolish* appear frequently in writings about slavery. To emancipate means "to set free" from slavery. To abolish means "to end slavery." An *abolitionist* was a person who wanted slavery to end.

- According to most estimates, 100,000 slaves escaped to the Northern states and Canada between 1810 and 1850.

- Born a slave, Frederick Douglass went on to become the most famous abolitionist. He said that slaves who free their minds by learning to read and to think as free people are no longer slaves, even though they are still in chains.

- Levi Coffin, a Quaker, was called the "president of the Underground Railroad." He helped more than 3,000 slaves escape.

- Harriet Tubman, herself a runaway slave, was a conductor on the Underground Railroad. There was a $40,000 reward for her capture, but Tubman was never caught.

- In 1852, Harriet Beecher Stowe finished her antislavery book entitled *Uncle Tom's Cabin*. In the first year alone, 300,000 copies were sold in America.

ABOUT
SLAVERY in AMERICA

Introduction

Many events led to the Civil War, but the most dramatic reason was the practice of slavery. Slavery was not new in the United States. African slaves were used for labor in the original thirteen colonies. Some of the United States' most respected leaders, including George Washington and Thomas Jefferson, were slave owners.

In the 1800s, many people in the Northern states began to think that slavery was morally wrong. By 1846, slavery was outlawed in all Northern states. The more the North protested the use of slavery, the more the South resisted.

The Life of a Slave

In the South, slaves were viewed as a large, cheap labor supply to raise cotton on plantations. The economy depended on growing and harvesting cotton. Slaves were considered property on the plantations. They could be sold and separated from their families at any time.

Slaves worked in the fields from sunrise to sunset. The conditions in which slaves lived were horrible. Six to twelve slaves slept in a single shack. Slaves were expected to obey their masters without question or face vicious beatings. Many slaves tried to escape, and some were successful. If caught, slaves were sent back to the plantations in chains.

The Abolitionist Movement

Throughout this period, the abolitionist movement grew in strength. Abolitionists had one common goal: to work together to end slavery in the United States. Famous abolitionists include Harriet Tubman, Sojourner Truth, Frederick Douglass, and John Brown.

The abolitionists wrote books, newspaper articles, pamphlets, and sermons that preached the evils of slavery. They also ran the "Underground Railroad." The Underground Railroad wasn't really a railroad. Instead, it was a nickname for the secret routes runaway slaves used to escape to the Northern states or to Canada.

A Nation Divided

The abolitionist movement angered pro-slavery Southerners. When Abraham Lincoln was elected in 1860, Southerners feared that he would abolish slavery nationwide. In 1861, eleven Southern states seceded, or withdrew, from the Union. That prompted the War Between the States.

The struggle for the abolition of slavery in America was a bloody one. It wasn't until 1865, when the Thirteenth Amendment to the Constitution was passed, that slavery was outlawed everywhere in the United States.

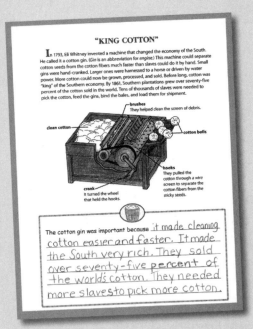

"KING COTTON"

Students read about the invention of the cotton gin and how it affected the need for slave labor in the production of cotton.

STEPS TO FOLLOW

1. Read and discuss "King Cotton" on page 19 with students.

2. Discuss the parts of the cotton gin and how it worked.

3. Direct students to write about the importance of the cotton gin during that period of history on the lines at the bottom of page 19.

4. Have students glue page 19 to the construction paper.

MATERIALS

- page 19, reproduced for each student
- 9" x 12" (23 x 30.5 cm) brown construction paper
- glue

"KING COTTON"

In 1793, Eli Whitney invented a machine that changed the economy of the South. He called it a cotton gin. (*Gin* is an abbreviation for *engine*.) This machine could separate cotton seeds from the cotton fibers much faster than slaves could do it by hand. Small gins were hand-cranked. Larger ones were harnessed to a horse or driven by water power. More cotton could now be grown, processed, and sold. Before long, cotton was "king" of the Southern economy. By 1861, Southern plantations grew over seventy-five percent of the cotton sold in the world. Tens of thousands of slaves were needed to pick the cotton, feed the gins, bind the bales, and load them for shipment.

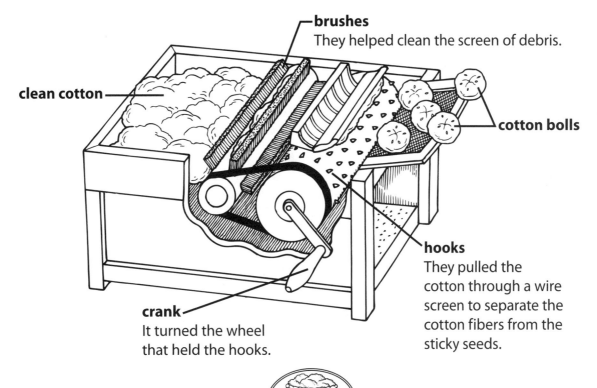

brushes
They helped clean the screen of debris.

clean cotton

cotton bolls

crank
It turned the wheel that held the hooks.

hooks
They pulled the cotton through a wire screen to separate the cotton fibers from the sticky seeds.

The cotton gin was important because _____

_____

_____

_____

_____

_____

THE SOUTHERN PLANTATION

All sorts of people lived and worked on a Southern plantation, including the planter, overseer, field slaves, and house slaves.

Students create an accordion-fold minibook that describes the different groups of people who worked on a Southern plantation at the time of the Civil War.

MATERIALS

- pages 21 and 22, reproduced for each student
- 6" x 18" (15 x 46 cm) colored construction paper
- ruler
- pencil
- colored pencils
- scissors
- glue

STEPS TO FOLLOW

1. Read about and discuss with students the different people who lived on a plantation. The information panels on page 21 are numbered in the sequence in which they should be read.

2. Guide students through the following steps to make the accordion-fold book:
   a. Measure 3" (7.5 cm) from one end of the construction paper. Make a mark on both the top and bottom edges.
   b. Use the ruler to connect the marks and draw a light pencil line.
   c. Fold on the line, and then fold back and forth as shown to create six panels.

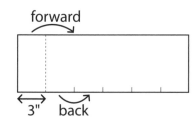

3. Next, instruct students to cut apart the information panels and the labels.

4. Students glue the title label to the first panel. Glue the introduction to the second panel. **Note:** Be sure to orient the book so that the panels open to the right.

5. Then have students match the information panels with the correct labels. Have them glue the sets to the remaining panels of the book and decorate using colored pencils.

INFORMATION PANELS

A plantation was a large farm in the South that specialized in growing one valuable crop such as cotton. A large plantation resembled a village. To keep a plantation running smoothly, each person had a set of jobs to do.

①

The owner of a plantation was called the planter. The planter was usually a wealthy, well-educated white man. The planter and his family lived in a mansion called the big house. Often the planter saw himself as a father figure for his slaves. Slaves were often forced to call him "master."

②

Most plantations had a few dozen slaves, but some of the largest had several hundred. Most of them were field slaves who worked in the fields picking cotton up to 14 hours a day. Men, women, and children were field slaves. They lived in one-room shacks behind the big house. Many large plantations also had workshops where skilled slaves worked. Skilled workers included blacksmiths, weavers, tailors, and shoemakers.

③

A few slaves lived in the big house. They were called house slaves. They cooked, cleaned, sewed, and looked after the planter's children. The slaves in the house ate better food and had nicer clothes than field slaves. House slaves worked hard to be on their best behavior. If they displeased the master or the mistress, they could be sent back to work in the fields.

④

The overseer supervised the work of field slaves. He kept them in line and made sure they worked hard. The overseer was usually a white man who worked for the planter. Slaves were terrified of the overseer because he often whipped and beat slaves to punish them or to make them work harder.

⑤

LABELS

The Planter

THE SOUTHERN PLANTATION

The Field Slaves and Other Workers

The House Slaves

The Overseer

VOICES OF PROTEST

In the 1800s, there were many people in the North, and some in the South, who protested the use of slavery. Some of the protesters were radical abolitionists like John Brown. Some worked for the Underground Railroad like the courageous Harriet Tubman. And others, like Frederick Douglass and Sojourner Truth, were magnificent orators who spoke out against slavery.

Students learn about these four antislavery leaders as they make a pop-up book highlighting their accomplishments.

STEPS TO FOLLOW

1. Read and discuss the information about the four leaders on page 25 with the students.

2. Show students how to cut and fold the construction paper to make the basic pop-up page, as shown. Have them repeat the process with all 4 pieces of construction paper.

  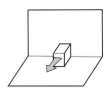

3. Have students color and cut out the four biographies, the labels and pictures, and the cover pattern.

4. Begin with the John Brown pop-up page.
   a. Glue the John Brown biography to the inside bottom panel.
   b. Glue the picture of John Brown to the pop-up tab.
   c. Glue the name and date label above the picture.

5. Repeat the process for the remaining pop-up pages.

6. Instruct students to glue the 4 pop-up pages together, laying one on top of another.

7. Then have students fold the cover pattern in half. Have them spread glue on the back of the cover pattern and wrap it around the outer folded edge of the pop-up book, with the title on the front.

MATERIALS

- pages 24–26, reproduced for each student
- four 6" x 9" (15 x 23 cm) pieces of colored construction paper
- colored pencils
- scissors
- glue

COVER PATTERN

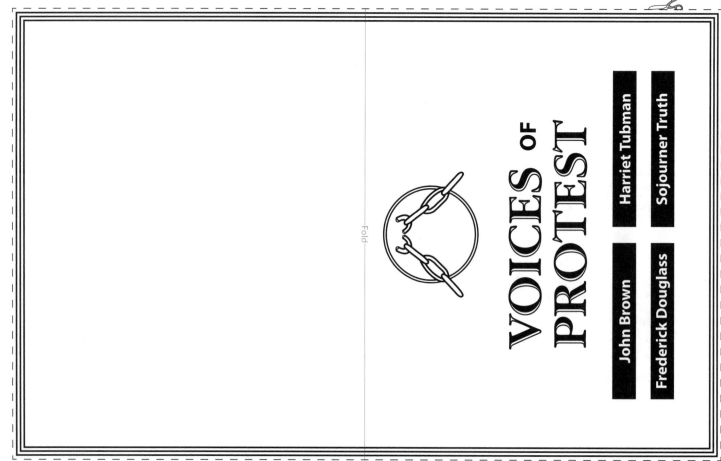

BIOGRAPHIES

Frederick Douglass, 1817–1895

- Douglass was born a slave. At age 8, he was sent to Maryland to work. He taught himself to read.
- In 1841, at a meeting of the Massachusetts Antislavery Society, Douglass gave a moving speech about what freedom meant to him. The society hired him to lecture about his experiences as a slave.
- In the early 1840s, Douglass protested against segregated seating on trains.
- In 1847, Douglass founded an antislavery newspaper entitled the *North Star*.
- Douglass's home was a station in the Underground Railroad.
- In the 1850s, Douglass spoke out against segregated schools and employers who hired white immigrants ahead of black Americans.

John Brown, 1800–1859

- As a young man, Brown helped fugitive slaves escape to Canada.
- In 1855, Brown moved to Kansas and worked to keep it from becoming a slave state. When proslavery men attacked and burned the town of Lawrence, Kansas, Brown led an expedition to kill five proslavery settlers.
- In 1859, Brown attacked Harpers Ferry, a government arsenal in West Virginia. He was hoping to arm slaves with guns from the arsenal and start a rebellion, but federal soldiers were sent to the fort to end the rebellion. Brown was tried for treason and executed. During the trial, he was quoted as saying that he believed God wanted him to end slavery with bloodshed.

Sojourner Truth, 1797–1883

- Truth was born a slave in New York. Her original name was Isabella Baumfree.
- In 1827, Truth ran away from her master and took refuge with an abolitionist family. She became free under a New York law that banned slavery.
- In 1843, she experienced what she thought was a command from God to preach. She took the name Sojourner Truth and began lecturing on the abolition of slavery.
- In 1864, Truth visited President Abraham Lincoln in the White House. She stayed in Washington, D.C., and helped find jobs and homes for slaves who had escaped from the South.

Harriet Tubman, 1820–1913

- Tubman was born a slave in Maryland.
- Tubman escaped from slavery in 1849 and went to Philadelphia using the Underground Railroad.
- During the 1850s, Tubman returned to the South 19 times and helped 300 slaves escape.
- During the Civil War, Tubman served as a nurse, a scout, and a spy for the Union army in South Carolina.
- After the war, Tubman raised money for black schools in New York.
- In 1908, Tubman established a home in New York for elderly and poor African Americans.
- Tubman is best known for her work with the Underground Railroad. She was quoted as saying: "I never ran my train off the track, and I never lost a passenger."

LABELS AND PICTURES

John Brown
1800–1859

Harriet Tubman
1820–1913

Frederick Douglass
1817–1895

Sojourner Truth
1797–1883

Pocket 3

LEADERS OF THE WAR

FAST FACTS

See page 2 for instructions on how to prepare
the Fast Facts bookmark and pocket label. As
you complete the activities in this pocket, read
the Fast Facts bookmark frequently for a quick
review.

ABOUT

Reproduce this page for students. Read and
discuss the information, incorporating available
library and multimedia resources. Refer to this
information page as you complete the activities
in this pocket.

ACTIVITIES

Students read about Abraham Lincoln and
Jefferson Davis. They make flip books describing
the highlights of each president's life. Then
students compare and contrast the men using
a Venn diagram.

Students read biographies of Ulysses S. Grant and
Robert E. Lee. Then they compare and contrast
the men using a Venn diagram. Students glue
the Venn diagram and the biographies onto
construction paper to make an informational
booklet.

LEADERS OF THE WAR

LEADERS OF THE WAR

FAST FACTS

- Both Abraham Lincoln and Jefferson Davis were born on farms in Kentucky.

- Both General Grant and General Lee graduated from the U.S. Military Academy at West Point in New York. Lee graduated with honors, while Grant was just an average student at the academy.

- President Lincoln asked Robert E. Lee to be field commander of all the Union armies. Lee chose to fight for his state of Virginia instead.

- Union General Grant respected Confederate General Lee. Grant was quoted as saying, "There was not a man in the Confederacy whose influence with the whole people was as great as his."

- In 1858, then-Congressman Abraham Lincoln gave Americans a warning in a speech: "A house divided against itself cannot stand. I believe this government cannot endure permanently half slave and have free... It will become all one thing, or all the other."

- Jefferson Davis's wife, Sarah, was the daughter of Zachary Taylor, an army general and president of the United States from 1849 to 1850.

ABOUT
LEADERS OF THE WAR

Abraham Lincoln

In 1860, Abraham Lincoln was elected as the sixteenth president of the United States. Shortly after the election, eleven Southern states seceded, an event that marked the beginning of the Civil War. For four years, Lincoln worked with Union generals to help ensure victory. He gave inspiring speeches, including the Gettysburg Address, delivered in 1863 at the site of the battle at Gettysburg. Lincoln also issued the Emancipation Proclamation, which declared freedom for all slaves living in the Confederacy. Because Lincoln did not have control of the South, the document did not free any slaves, but it did send a message—slavery would be outlawed when the Union won. In 1864, Lincoln was elected to a second term. Less than a week after the war ended in 1865, Lincoln was shot to death by John Wilkes Booth. Because he saved the Union and ended slavery, many people consider Abraham Lincoln the greatest of all presidents.

Jefferson Davis

When the South seceded, Jefferson Davis hoped he would be in charge of the Confederate army. Instead, he was named president of the Confederate States of America. Davis ran the government from its capital in Richmond, Virginia. Davis was an experienced soldier. He had also been a U.S. congressman, senator, and secretary of war. Davis was a champion of states' rights. As a leader of the Confederacy, he was a good administrator. But he proved to be a poor planner. He had difficulties with his Congress and was considered inflexible. When the war ended, Davis was taken prisoner. A grand jury indicted him for treason, but he never stood trial. Instead, he was released on bail. Davis spent his last years writing about his war experiences.

Ulysses S. Grant

General Ulysses S. Grant commanded the Union army from 1864 to 1865. He was considered a brilliant leader. He was very successful in leading battles in the western portion of the country. In 1863, Grant and his troops captured Vicksburg, a key location on the Mississippi River. By 1865, his Union forces proved to be too strong for the Confederate army. Grant accepted General Lee's surrender at Appomattox Court House, Virginia, to end the war. Grant went on to become the eighteenth president of the United States.

Robert E. Lee

The son of a Revolutionary War hero, General Robert E. Lee was considered the greatest officer in the war. Even though he opposed slavery and secession, he chose to fight for his home state of Virginia. Lee led the Confederacy to important victories in the Second Battle of Bull Run and at Fredericksburg and Chancellorsville, but lost at Gettysburg and eventually surrendered at Appomattox Court House on April 9, 1865.

MATERIALS

- pages 31–33, reproduced for each student
- two 9" x 10" (23 x 25.5 cm) sheets of colored construction paper
- colored pencils
- scissors
- glue

THE PRESIDENTS

Students read about Abraham Lincoln and Jefferson Davis to learn about the men who led the North and South during the Civil War. Students make flip books describing highlights of the lives of each of the presidents.

STEPS TO FOLLOW

1. As a class, read the biographies of both men on pages 31 and 32. Review page 29 for additional information.

2. Have students color and cut out the information and illustrations on pages 31 and 32. **Note:** The information and the illustrations are each one piece.

3. Next, students fold two sheets of construction paper in half as shown.

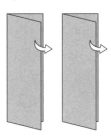

4. Then students glue the information about each president to the front of the folded pieces of construction paper.

5. Have students cut on the dark bold lines, only cutting through the top layer of the construction paper folders to create three flaps.

6. Then students glue the picture panel inside on the right-hand side, as shown.

7. As a class, fill in the Venn diagram on page 33 to compare and contrast the two presidents.

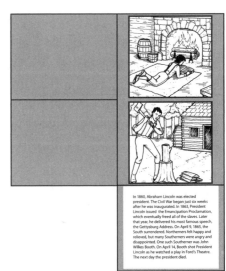

ABRAHAM LINCOLN
1809–1865
President of the United States

Abraham Lincoln was born in a log cabin in Kentucky on February 12, 1809. He later described the land as a "wild region, where many bears and animals still roamed." When Lincoln was seven, his family moved to Indiana. Three years later, his mother died. Like many country boys, Lincoln did not have much formal schooling. His days were filled with farm chores. But at night, Lincoln taught himself by candlelight from borrowed books.

As a young man, Lincoln had many jobs. He was a railsplitter, boatman, and storekeeper. He fought Native Americans during the Black Hawk War. Afterward, he moved to Springfield, Illinois, and became a lawyer. He was so well-liked that people nicknamed him "Honest Abe." In 1842, Lincoln married Mary Todd. Both of them believed that slavery was wrong. Lincoln once said, "Whenever I hear anyone arguing for slavery, I feel a strong impulse to see it tried on him personally."

In 1860, Abraham Lincoln was elected president. The Civil War began just six weeks after he was inaugurated. In 1863, President Lincoln issued the Emancipation Proclamation, which eventually freed all of the slaves. Later that year, he delivered his most famous speech, the Gettysburg Address. On April 9, 1865, the South surrendered. Northerners felt happy and relieved, but many Southerners were angry and disappointed. One such Southerner was John Wilkes Booth. On April 14, Booth shot President Lincoln as he watched a play in Ford's Theatre. The next day, the president died.

JEFFERSON DAVIS
1808–1899
President of the Confederate States of America

Davis was born in Kentucky on June 3, 1808. At 16, he entered the U.S. Military Academy, graduating in 1828. Davis served in the army for seven years. He fought in campaigns against Indians, and took charge of the Indian removal after the Black Hawk War. In 1835, Davis married Sarah Taylor. They moved to Mississippi to manage his cotton plantation. When his wife died, Davis traveled for a year and studied the U.S. Constitution. He continued to manage his plantation and became wealthy.

Davis became a U.S. congressman in 1845. That same year, he married Varina Howell. He resigned from Congress in 1846 to become a colonel in a regiment of Mississippi volunteers in the Mexican War. In 1847, the governor of Mississippi appointed Davis to fill out the term of a U.S. senator who had died. In 1850, Davis resigned from the senate to run for governor. He lost the election and retired to his plantation. In 1853, President Pierce appointed him secretary of war. After his term expired, Davis was reelected to the Senate and served as a spokesman for the South. He believed strongly in states' rights and demanded that Congress protect slavery.

After Abraham Lincoln was elected president, the state of Mississippi seceded from the Union. Davis resigned from the Senate again, and was named president of the Confederate States of America. As president, he insisted on a strategy of defending all Southern territory equally, which was too expensive. This strategy also allowed Union forces to hit hard in vulnerable areas such as New Orleans and Atlanta. When the South lost the war, Davis was taken prisoner. A grand jury indicted him for treason, and he was held in prison for two years, awaiting trial. A Northerner paid his bail, and Davis was released. He was never tried.

TWO LEADERS

Fill in this Venn diagram to compare the Union and Confederate presidents during the Civil War.

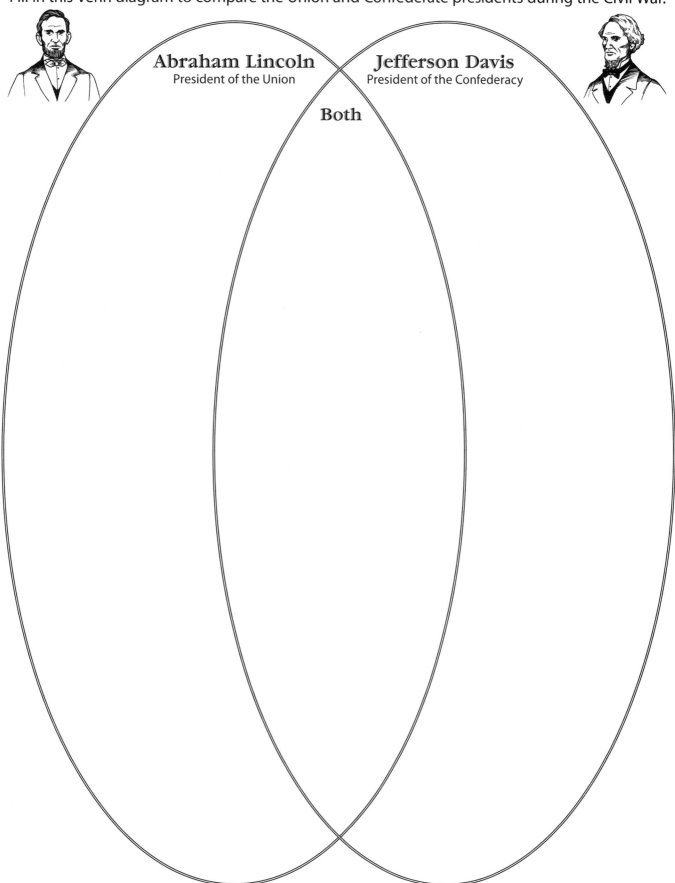

Abraham Lincoln
President of the Union

Jefferson Davis
President of the Confederacy

Both

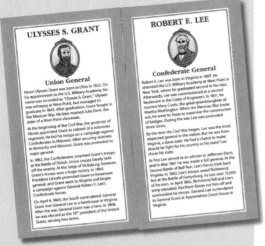

TWO GREAT GENERALS

Generals Ulysses S. Grant and Robert E. Lee became celebrated throughout America for their strong leadership during the Civil War. While the men had some things in common, there were some major differences, as well.

Students read about the Civil War's most famous generals. Then they compare and contrast the two men using a Venn diagram.

MATERIALS

- pages 35 and 36, reproduced for each student
- 8" x 18" (20 x 46 cm) colored construction paper
- pencils or pens
- scissors
- glue

STEPS TO FOLLOW

1. Read the biographies of Grant and Lee as a class, in small groups, or individually. Also refer back to the information presented on page 29.

2. Distribute the Venn diagram on page 36. Discuss with students the similarities of the two men. Ideas include such things as: Both graduated from West Point. Both were generals. Have students write at least two similarities on the overlapping circle on the diagram.

3. Then instruct students to write the differences between the two men on the diagram. Encourage them to write at least four differences. You may choose to do this as a class, in small groups, or individually.

4. When the Venn diagram is complete, have students share their answers with the class.

5. Have students fold the construction paper as shown.

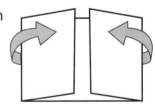

6. Students then glue the biographies of the generals on the outside flaps. Have them cut out the Venn diagram and glue it on the inside panel.

ULYSSES S. GRANT

Union General

Hiram Ulysses Grant was born in Ohio in 1822. On his appointment to the U.S. Military Academy, his name was recorded as "Ulysses S. Grant." Ulysses was unhappy at West Point, but managed to graduate in 1843. After graduation, Grant fought in the Mexican War. He later married Julia Dent, the sister of a West Point classmate.

At the beginning of the Civil War, the governor of Illinois appointed Grant as colonel of a volunteer regiment. He led his troops on a campaign against Confederates in Missouri. After securing victories in Kentucky and Missouri, Grant was promoted to major general.

In 1862, the Confederates surprised Grant's troops at the Battle of Shiloh. Union troops barely held off the enemy. At the Siege of Vicksburg, however, Grant's troops won a huge victory. In 1864, President Lincoln promoted Grant to lieutenant general, and Grant went to Virginia and began a campaign against General Robert E. Lee's Confederate forces.

On April 9, 1865, the South surrendered. General Grant met General Lee in a farmhouse in Virginia. After the war, General Grant was a hero. In 1868, he was elected as the eighteenth president of the United States, serving two terms.

ROBERT E. LEE

Confederate General

Robert E. Lee was born in Virginia in 1807. He attended the U.S. Military Academy at West Point in New York, where he graduated second in his class. Afterwards, Lee was commissioned as a second lieutenant in the Corps of Engineers. In 1831, he married Mary Custis, the great-granddaughter of Martha Washington. When the Mexican War broke out, he went to Texas to supervise the construction of bridges. During the war, Lee was promoted three times.

By the time the Civil War began, Lee was the most respected general in the nation. But he was from Virginia, a slave state. He had a choice to make: should he fight for his country or his state? Lee chose his state.

At first, Lee served as an adviser to Jefferson Davis, and in May 1861 he was made a full general. At the Second Battle of Bull Run, Lee's forces took back Virginia. In 1862, Lee's troops saved Richmond, but at the Battle of Gettysburg, he lost over 12,000 of his men. In April 1865, Richmond fell and Lee's army retreated. Northern forces cut him off and surrounded his troops. General Lee surrendered to General Grant at Appomattox Court House in Virginia.

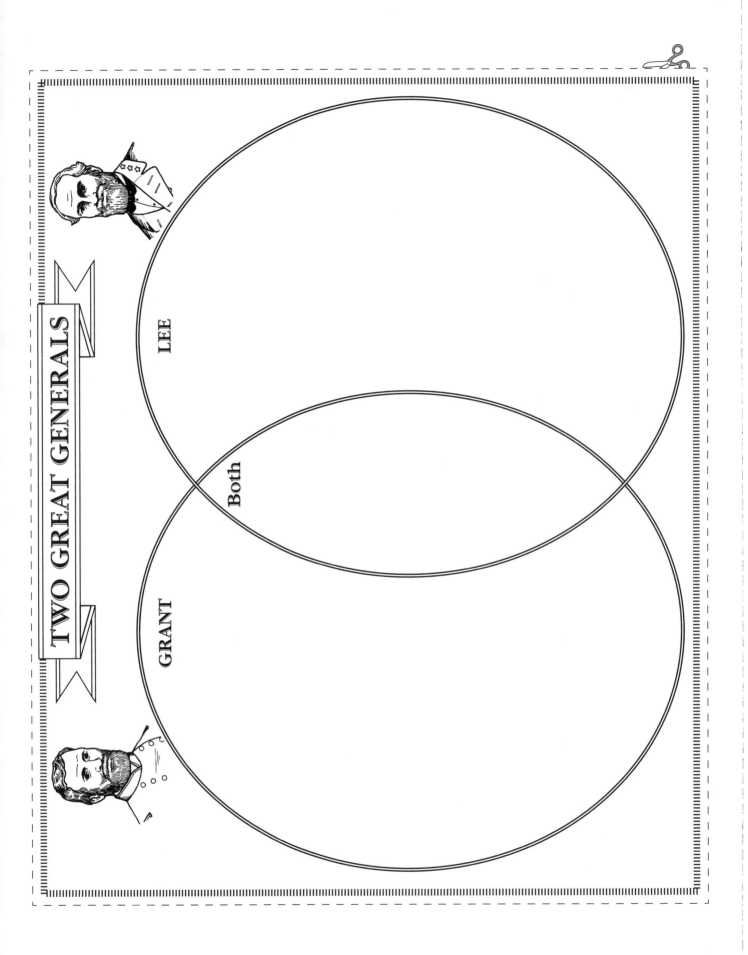

TWO GREAT GENERALS

LEE

Both

GRANT

Pocket 4
MAJOR BATTLES

FAST FACTS

See page 2 for instructions on how to prepare the Fast Facts bookmark and pocket label. As you complete the activities in this pocket, read the Fast Facts bookmark frequently for a quick review.

ABOUT

Reproduce this page for students. Read and discuss the information, incorporating available library and multimedia resources. Refer to this information page as you complete the activities in this pocket.

ACTIVITIES

Students read about and discuss the attack on Fort Sumter, the First Battle of Bull Run, the Battle of Gettysburg, and Sherman's March to the Sea. They also read the text of the Gettysburg Address, the speech that Abraham Lincoln delivered shortly after that bloody battle. Students make a booklet telling the who, what, where, and when of each battle.

MAJOR BATTLES

MAJOR BATTLES
FAST FACTS

- The American Civil War consisted of more than 50 major battles and 5,000 minor battles.

- Many battles had two names. The Southerners named them after the nearest settlements. The Northerners named each battle after the nearest body of water.

- A small U.S. flag flew over Fort Sumter during the first battle of the war. A Southern shell knocked it down. Under fire, a Union sergeant climbed the flagpole and nailed it back into place. The tattered flag was lowered when the Union soldiers surrended the fort.

- The Battle of Gettysburg was the largest battle ever fought in North America.

- When the Union army retreated at the First Battle of Bull Run, they ran into hundreds of civilians who had come out to witness the battle. The road back to Washington became a tangled mess of troops, horses, and frightened people in carriages.

- Cannons were the deadliest weapons in the war. The most common cannon was the Model 1857 gun-howitzer. Soldiers called it a "Napoleon." It was named after Louis Napoléon, the ruler of France at the time. The ruler had sponsored the development of this gun.

ABOUT
MAJOR BATTLES

Introduction

At the beginning of the American Civil War, most Northerners did not think that the war would last longer than three months. After all, the North was larger and stronger. But when the Confederates won battles early on, people realized that the war was going to be a long and bloody struggle.

The Appalachian Mountains divided the war into two main theaters, or military areas. The Western Theater was located between the mountains and the Mississippi River. The Eastern Theater stretched from the mountains east to the Atlantic Ocean. A smaller military area west of the Mississippi River saw some minor action.

The Eastern Front

Major battles on the eastern front mostly took place in Maryland, Pennsylvania, and Virginia. Famous battles which the South won were: the First Battle of Bull Run, the Second Battle of Bull Run, the Battle of Chancellorsville, the Battle of Seven Days, and the Battle of Fredericksburg. Decisive victories for the North included the Battle of Gettysburg, the Battle of Antietam, and the Battle of Petersburg.

The Western Front

Major battles on the western front occurred in Tennessee and along the Mississippi River. The Northern forces dominated this theater, winning such famous battles as the Battle of Chattanooga, the Battle of Shiloh, and the Siege of Vicksburg. The Battle of Chickamauga, fought in 1863, was the Confederacy's last major victory of the war.

A Battle of Wills

In the final year of the war, the troops of Union General Ulysses S. Grant and Confederate General Robert E. Lee met several times on the battlefields.

In May 1864, in the Battle of the Wilderness, both men's troops suffered major losses and neither could claim victory. Grant was determined to win, though. He pushed toward Richmond, the Confederate capital.

At the Battle of Spotsylvania Court House, the armies of Grant and Lee fought again. There was no victory for either side.

At the Battle of Cold Harbor, just north of Richmond, Virginia, the two generals sent their troops into battle yet again. About 50,000 Union troops attacked 30,000 Confederate soldiers, who were in trenches. Grant lost 12,000 men that day. In June 1864, at the Siege of Petersburg, Virginia, Grant finally pinned down Lee's troops.

Surrender

When fighting on other fronts weakened the South even further, General Lee knew the cause was lost. On April 9, 1865, the two great generals met at Appomattox Court House in Virginia. General Lee surrendered to General Grant, and the war was officially over.

CIVIL WAR BATTLES

The Civil War had many important battles and events. Some of the most significant include the attack on Fort Sumter, the First Battle of Bull Run, the Battle of Gettysburg, and Sherman's March to the Sea.

Students build a book with pull-up tabs that summarize the important facts about these battles. They also read Lincoln's Gettysburg Address, presented at a ceremony to dedicate part of the battlefield as a cemetery.

Note: This project will require several class periods.

MATERIALS

- page 41, reproduce four copies for each student
- pages 42–47, reproduced for each student
- 9" x 12" (23 x 30.5 cm) red construction paper
- 12" x 18" (30.5 x 46 cm) red construction paper
- pencil
- crayons or colored pencils
- scissors
- glue
- hole punch
- metal rings or yarn

STEPS TO FOLLOW

1. As a class, read about each of the four battles (pages 43–45 and 47). Locate each one on the map (page 42), then discuss and highlight the 4 Ws—the who, what, where, and when of each battle.

2. Distribute 4 copies of the form on page 41 to each student. Students write the name of a battle on each form. Then they use the information provided to complete the form.

3. Distribute page 46 and read Lincoln's Gettysburg Address to students. Define vocabulary such as "conceived in Liberty" and "consecrate." Explain Lincoln's words in simpler language.

4. Direct students to cut out each of the pull-tab forms and the information pages.

5. Demonstrate how to cut on the cut lines at the top of each information page. Show students how to slip each pull-tab form through the slit in its corresponding sheet.

6. Then have students fold the large sheet of construction page in half to form a folder and insert the smaller sheet of construction paper in the center of the folder.

7. Next, students color, cut out, and glue the map to the front of the folder.

8. Instruct students to apply glue to the outside edge of the Fort Sumter information page with its pull-tab form inserted, then place it on the inside front cover of the folder.

9. Students then glue the remaining pages in this order: Battle of Bull Run, Battle of Gettysburg, Gettysburg Address, and Sherman's March to the Sea.

10. Have students hole punch and bind their books with metal rings or yarn.

Step 5

Pull-Tab Form

_____
Battle

WHO: _____

WHAT: _____

WHERE: _____

WHEN: _____

RESULT: _____

_____

_____

_____

_____

_____

_____

N

Gettysburg, PA

Bull Run
Manassas, Virginia

Atlanta

Fort Sumter
Charleston, South Carolina

Savannah

SHERMAN'S MARCH TO THE SEA,
from Atlanta to Savannah, Georgia

CIVIL WAR BATTLES

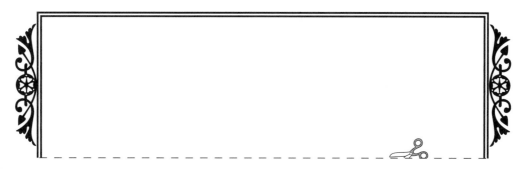

Fort Sumter was a U.S. fort located on an island in the harbor of Charleston, South Carolina. The fort was commanded by Major Robert Anderson.

When South Carolina seceded in 1860, the Union claimed the fort as U.S. property. The Confederacy thought it was part of its new country and wanted the Union men out. Confederate officials ordered Major Anderson to evacuate the fort. Anderson sent messages to Lincoln that he had only a six-week supply of food. Lincoln chose to send warships to resupply the fort. The Confederate officials saw this as a threat.

Before the Federal warships could reach Charleston, Anderson was again asked to surrender. When the major refused, President Davis ordered Southern forces to open fire.

At 4:30 a.m. on April 12, 1861, Fort Sumter became the site of the first shot fired in the Civil War. The next day, heavy cannon fire set the fort on fire. Major Anderson's men tried to defend it, but they were outnumbered. After 34 hours of shelling, Major Anderson surrendered the fort. Amazingly, neither side lost a man during the artillery fire.

The Federal flag was lowered on the afternoon of April 12. Fort Sumter remained under Confederate control until the war ended.

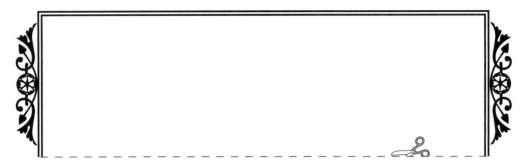

On July 21, 1861, the **First Battle of Bull Run** was fought. It was the first major land battle of the Civil War. Confederates called it the Battle of Manassas, after the town of Manassas along the Bull Run Creek in Virginia.

Union General Irvin McDowell's inexperienced army of 28,000 soldiers advanced on Confederate General P.G.T. Beauregard's smaller forces. But before McDowell could attack, General Joseph Johnston's Confederate troops arrived to provide reinforcement for Beauregard's men.

The North launched several attacks, and it looked as if the Union army was going to break through the Confederate lines. During one attack, the troops of Confederate General Thomas Jackson held their ground so strongly that Jackson earned the nickname "Stonewall."

After stopping the Union attacks, the Confederates counterattacked, and the Union troops were forced to retreat to Washington, D.C. General McDowell was blamed for the Union loss in the First Battle of Bull Run and was replaced by General George McClellan.

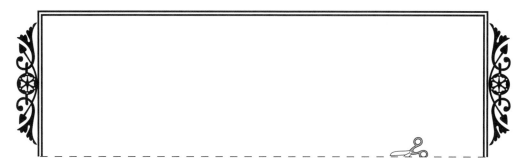

$\mathbb{T}$he **Battle of Gettysburg** occurred from July 1 to July 3, 1863, near the town of Gettysburg, Pennsylvania. Fighting broke out when Confederate troops ran into Union cavalry west of Gettysburg. General Robert E. Lee rushed 25,000 soldiers to Gettysburg, and the Union army was pushed back. They regrouped, though, and 80,000 additional Union soldiers arrived that night.

On July 2, General Lee's offensive began. In the late afternoon and into the evening, bloody battles were waged. Confederate troops made several assaults, but they were met with heavy Union fire. By the end of the day, neither army had made much headway.

On July 3, General Lee ordered Confederate cannons to open fire to help pave the way for about 15,000 soldiers to storm the hill. To fool the Confederates into thinking their cannons were knocked out, the Union army ceased firing. The Confederates charged across an open field, and Union cannons and rifle volleys killed many of them. The remaining Confederate soldiers charged ahead, and there was a fierce hand-to-hand fight. The Confederates were pushed back down the hill.

The tide of the war turned that day, but the Northern victory came at a terrible price. Confederate casualties in dead, wounded, and missing soldiers were more than 25,000. Union casualties were about 23,000 men.

The Gettysburg Address

President Abraham Lincoln delivered this speech on November 19, 1863, at ceremonies to dedicate a part of the Gettysburg battlefield as a cemetery for those who had lost their lives in the battle. This speech is among the best remembered in American history.

Four score and seven years ago our fathers brought forth on this continent, a new nation, conceived in Liberty, and dedicated to the proposition that all men are created equal.

Now we are engaged in a great civil war, testing whether that nation, or any nation so conceived and so dedicated, can long endure. We are met on a great battlefield of that war. We have come to dedicate a portion of that field, as a final resting place for those who here gave their lives that that nation might live. It is altogether fitting and proper that we should do this.

But, in a larger sense, we can not dedicate—we can not consecrate—we can not hallow—this ground. The brave men living and dead, who struggled here, have consecrated it, far above our poor power to add or detract. The world will little note, nor long remember, what we say here, but it can never forget what they did here. It is for us the living, rather, to be dedicated here to the unfinished work which they who fought here have thus far so nobly advanced. It is rather for us to be here dedicated to the great task remaining before us—that from these honored dead we take increased devotion to that cause for which they gave the last full measure of devotion—that we here highly resolve that these dead shall not have died in vain—that this nation, under God, shall have a new birth of freedom—and that government of the people, by the people, for the people, shall not perish from the earth.

The American Civil War • EMC 3724 • © Evan-Moor Corp.

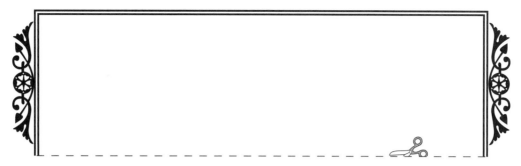

Having taken occupation of Atlanta and forcibly evacuated the city's residents, Union General William T. Sherman and his 62,000 troops began the **March to the Sea** in November 1864. Sherman's army marched in two columns 25 to 60 miles wide from Atlanta to the port of Savannah. They destroyed railroads, bridges, telegraph lines, manufacturing plants, and plantations along the way.

Sherman's army was so large that it faced little resistance. When they reached Savannah, they met 10,000 Confederate soldiers who were defending the port. Following a lengthy artillery battle, Confederate General William J. Hardee abandoned the city. Sherman entered the port on December 22, 1864.

From Savannah, Sherman marched north through the Carolinas to meet General Grant's troops. Along the way, Sherman's troops continued the policy of "slash-and-burn." This meant that they seized or destroyed all important property along their path.

General Sherman's slash-and-burn policy has always been controversial. Some historians think his military strategy was excellent. He destroyed the Confederacy's ability to wage further battle, and that hastened the end of the war. Others find the policy too destructive to civilian life. To burn crops, kill livestock, and destroy homes should not be a military objective.

Pocket 5

A SOLDIER'S LIFE

FAST FACTS

See page 2 for instructions on how to prepare the Fast Facts bookmark and pocket label. As you complete the activities in this pocket, read the Fast Facts bookmark frequently for a quick review.

ABOUT

Reproduce this page for students. Read and discuss the information, incorporating available library and multimedia resources. Refer to this page as you complete the activities in this pocket.

ACTIVITIES

Students learn about Civil War uniforms and equipment. They color Union and Confederate soldiers, labeling items on the drawings, and glue the information and pictures to construction paper.

Students learn about the variety of uniforms worn by both Union and Confederate troops and make accordion-fold displays that show the uniforms.

Students create a battle drum booklet and draw what they would have hidden inside their drum. Information about a real drummer boy fills the rest of the booklet.

Students read a made-up letter from a soldier, write a response, and construct an envelope for the letter.

Students learn about the types of food that soldiers ate and assemble their own cookbook of Civil War recipes.

Students create their own model of a pup tent. They discuss and write about what life must have been like for the soldiers living in these conditions.

A SOLDIER'S LIFE

A SOLDIER'S LIFE

FAST FACTS

- Union soldiers nicknamed Confederate soldiers "butternuts" because their light gray uniforms often faded to brown.

- About 180,000 black soldiers served in the Union army. Two-thirds of them were Southerners who had fled to freedom in the North.

- Boys as young as 9 years old tried to join the army. Most were sent home, but some stayed on as drummer boys.

- A thin flour biscuit called hardtack was a common part of a food ration for soldiers. They renamed the biscuits "tooth-dullers," "worm castles," and "sheet iron crackers."

- During the winter months, soldiers would build log huts. Soldiers often named their huts after restaurants and hotels at home, such as "Wiltshire Hotel" or "Madigan's Oyster House."

- Even though it was against orders, soldiers kept pets such as dogs, cats, squirrels, and raccoons. One Wisconsin regiment had a pet eagle that was carried on its own perch.

ABOUT
A SOLDIER'S LIFE

Reasons for Joining

Throughout the Civil War, huge numbers of men and boys on both sides signed up to fight. Northern soldiers felt that the South had no right to leave the Union. Confederate soldiers felt they were defending their homeland. Some young men joined the fight simply because they thought it would be a great adventure. Most were disappointed to learn that life as a soldier was very different than what they had imagined.

Day-to-Day Life

Military service meant many months away from home. There were long hours of drill and practice. Strict discipline was the order of the day. Loaded down with equipment, infantry soldiers had to practice marching and loading their muskets over and over again. Cavalrymen drilled both on foot and on horseback. Artillerymen drilled with their cannons. Musicians practiced their marching music.

Mail was one of the few things that soldiers had to look forward to in camp. Many soldiers spent the afternoons writing letters. Some kept diaries. Soldiers loved receiving letters from family and friends, but mail delivery was slow and unreliable. Sometimes, writing supplies were so scarce that soldiers learned to make ink from wild berries.

In the Union army, tent camps were set up during the mild months of the year. A two-man tent was called a pup tent. Men joked that only a dog could crawl under it and stay dry. Mostly, Confederate soldiers did not receive shelter tents. For long winter sieges, Union soldiers built log huts.

Boring weeks of camp life were interrupted regularly by terrifying days, weeks, and even months of battles with the enemy.

A Soldier's Diet

There were similarities in the diets of soldiers on both sides. Pork or beef and bread were common rations for a Union soldier. Other food items included rice, peas, beans, dried fruit, potatoes, and salt. Coffee and sugar were the products Union soldiers thought most desirable. Confederate soldiers lived on a diet of beef or pork, cornmeal, peas, and rice.

Often, supply trains on both sides were delayed. Some food arrived stale, rotten, or full of insects. Soldiers learned to fend for themselves by hunting small animals, picking berries, and taking vegetables from nearby gardens.

Staying Healthy

Sickness and disease plagued both armies. In fact, twice as many men died of disease than in battle. Smallpox, diphtheria, dysentery, measles, yellow fever, and malaria were some of the most common diseases. Camp doctors and nurses were kept busy with the sick and wounded.

  The American Civil War • EMC 3724 • © Evan-Moor Corp.

CIVIL WAR INFANTRY UNIFORMS

Both armies issued uniforms to their soldiers. Union soldiers wore blue and Confederate soldiers wore gray. The soldiers had to carry heavy equipment as they marched to war.

Students read about the uniforms of the Union and Confederate infantrymen, and then make folded display forms that show the uniform parts and equipment.

STEPS TO FOLLOW

1. With students, read about the uniforms and equipment of Union and Confederate infantrymen on pages 52 and 53. As each item is read, have students locate it on the illustration. If an item is not labeled on the illustration, students are to add their own label.

2. Have students color the uniforms, using the information as their guide.

3. Students cut out the titles, the informational text, and the illustrations of both the Union and the Confederate uniforms.

4. Demonstrate how to fold each of the construction paper strips as shown.

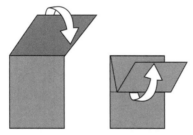

5. Students then glue the titles, informational text, and illustrations to the construction paper strips.

MATERIALS

- pages 52 and 53, reproduced for each student

- two 6" x 18" (15 x 46 cm) pieces of colored construction paper

- crayons, colored pencils, or marking pens

- scissors

- glue

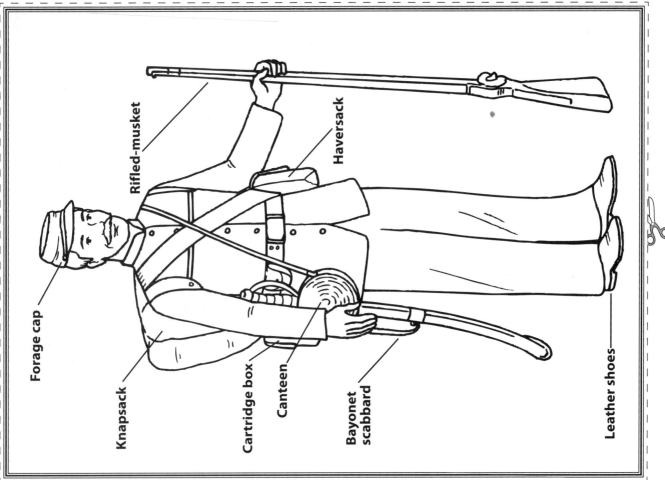

Labels on diagram:
- Rifled-musket
- Haversack
- Forage cap
- Knapsack
- Cartridge box
- Canteen
- Bayonet scabbard
- Leather shoes

Uniform:

- Navy blue wool jacket and trousers
- Blue forage cap made of wool broadcloth with a flat, rounded top, cotton lining, and a leather visor
- Wool flannel shirt
- Wool socks
- Leather shoes

Equipment:

- Almost fifty pounds of equipment
- A bag called a haversack held the soldier's food rations.
- A knapsack stored personal items, a blanket, and a tent. Like the haversack, it was made of canvas and was waterproof.
- The Union soldier's canteen was superior to the Confederate soldier's. It was made of tin with a pewter spout and cork. It was covered with a cotton and wool cloth that kept the water cool.
- Rifled-musket, leather scabbard for bayonet, forty cartridges of ammunition

UNION INFANTRY SOLDIER'S UNIFORM

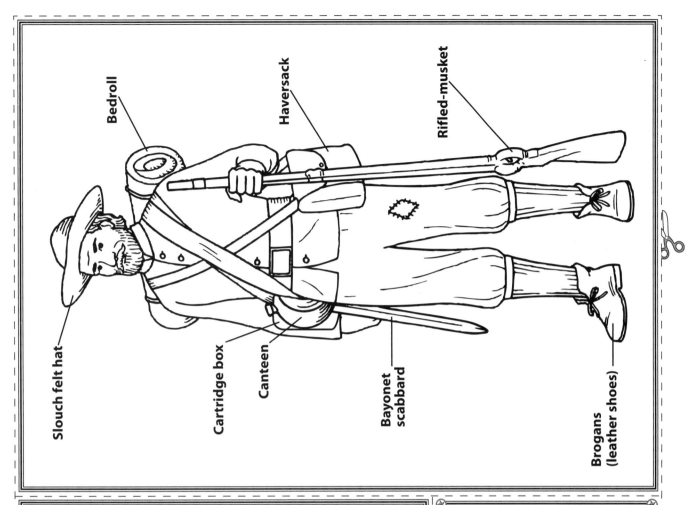

Bedroll

Haversack

Rifled-musket

Slouch felt hat

Cartridge box

Canteen

Bayonet scabbard

Brogans (leather shoes)

Uniform:

- Gray short-waisted jacket
- Trousers
- Light cotton or flannel underwear
- Wool shirt
- Jacket and trousers were made of a coarse material called jean, which was cotton and wool blended together.
- Gray forage cap or broad-brimmed slouch felt hat
- Confederate-made shoes, called brogans, were not good. Some men were forced to go barefoot until good shoes could be found.
- Cotton haversack
- Thin tin canteen
- Bedroll

Equipment:

- The Confederate soldier carried his rifle and the scabbard for his bayonet. He also had to carry forty cartridges of ammunition.

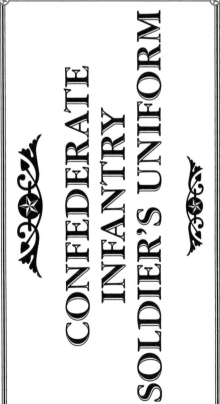

CONFEDERATE INFANTRY SOLDIER'S UNIFORM

A PARADE OF UNIFORMS

At the beginning of the Civil War, there was no standard uniform for the soldiers. As a result, both Union and Confederate forces had many different uniforms in use, some of them very colorful and exotic looking. As the war progressed, both armies adopted a more standard uniform to avoid confusion.

Students make accordion-fold displays to show the variety of uniforms worn by soldiers of both armies during the Civil War.

MATERIALS

- pages 55–57, reproduced for each student
- two 6" x 18" (15 x 46 cm) pieces of colored construction paper
- colored pencils or fine-tip marking pens
- ruler
- pencil
- scissors
- glue

STEPS TO FOLLOW

1. Discuss the different uniforms featured on pages 55 and 56.

2. Instruct students to color the uniforms using the information on the chart on page 57. Tell students that when a uniform part is not described, they should use their best judgment as to an appropriate color.

3. Guide students through the following steps to make the accordion-fold displays:

   a. Measure 3" (7.5 cm) from one end of the construction paper. Make a mark on both the top and bottom edges.

   b. Use the ruler to connect the marks and draw a light pencil line.

   c. Fold on the line, and then fold back and forth as shown to create six panels.

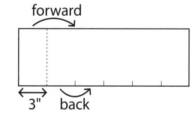

4. Next, students cut out the title and Union uniforms and glue each to a section of the folded strip of paper. They glue the Confederate title and uniforms to the other strip.

A PARADE OF UNIFORMS

Union Soldiers
by

_____

_____

Mule Driver

Captain from Rhode Island

Quartermaster, U.S. Navy

New York Zouave

U.S. Marine Captain

A PARADE OF UNIFORMS

Confederate Soldiers
by

_____

_____

2nd Lieut., Confederate
Marine Corps

1st Lieut., South Carolina

Major, Medical Dept.

Private, Virginia Cavalry

Virginia Militia Volunteer

☆ UNIFORM GUIDELINES ☆

rank/title	hat	shirt	vest	jacket	trousers	boots/shoes	other
Union Soldiers							
Mule driver	brown	red	Green and white stripes	light gray	light blue	black	—
Captain from Rhode Island	dark blue with a brass hunting horn insignia	—	—	dark blue with brass buttons	light blue	black	gray canteen with brown strap; buff gauntlets (gloves); black belt
Quartermaster, U.S. Navy	dark blue with black band	—	—	dark blue with white stripes on collar and cuffs	dark blue or white	black	black tie
New York Zouave (*zwahv*)	white with blue tassel	dark blue with red trim	—	dark blue with red trim	red	black with white gaiters	dark blue sash with light blue edging
U.S. Marine Captain	dark blue with yellow pompom	—	—	dark blue with yellow collar, cuffs, and trim	white	black	white belt
Confederate Soldiers							
2nd Lieutenant, Confederate Marine Corp	gray	white	gray	gray with gold designs and black trim; brass buttons	gray, dark blue, or white	black	black tie
1st Lieutenant, South Carolina	brown with red feather	—	—	gray with yellow collar, cuffs, and trim	light blue	black	black belt; tan gloves
Major, Medical Department	gray	—	—	gray with black trim; gold braid; brass buttons	light blue with black and gold stripes	black	green sash
Private, Virginia Cavalry	black	—	green	gray with yellow trim and brass buttons	gray	brown	brown holster; brass sword hilt and scabbard
Virginia Militia Volunteer	dark blue with red stripe and tassel	red checks	—	gray with dark blue trim	yellow-brown	brown	brown shoulder belts; black waist belt

THE DRUMMER BOY

Even though the legal age to enlist was eighteen, over 250,000 Civil War soldiers were sixteen years old or younger. Both armies had rules that banned young boys from enlisting, but birth certificates were rare. Armies made exceptions by letting younger boys become drummers. The drummer boy was an important part of each troop. Different drumbeats stood for different orders, such as when to report for battle. It was common for boys to draw checkerboards on the head, or top, of their drum. The drum heads unscrewed, so boys could store their favorite things inside the shell of the drum.

Students create their own battle drum booklet. Then they draw what they would have hidden inside the shell of the drum if they had been drummer boys. They fill the rest of the booklet with information about a real drummer boy who served in the Civil War.

MATERIALS

- pages 59 and 60, reproduced for each student
- 9" x 12" (23 x 30.5 cm) light-colored construction paper
- scissors
- glue
- pencil
- crayons, colored pencils, or marking pens

STEPS TO FOLLOW

1. As a class, read about drummer boys on page 59. Ask students to think of a special object that they would have stored inside their drums if they were drummer boys.

2. Direct students to fold the construction paper in half as shown to create a four-page booklet.

3. Have students color and decorate the drum pattern on page 59. They cut it out and fold back the tab. Then they glue the tab to the front cover of the booklet.

4. Have students lift the drum pattern and draw the item they would store in their drums.

5. As a class, read about Johnny Clem on page 60. Students then cut out his picture and biography and glue them on the inside pages of the booklet.

6. Finally, students glue the information about drummer boys on the back cover.

THE DRUMMER BOY

Drummer boys were very important to a troop. Their drumbeats communicated orders to the soldiers. For example, one drumbeat told soldiers to report for drill time, where they would practice marching and loading and unloading their weapons. The "long roll" was a signal for the soldiers to march into battle. A "rally" drumbeat ordered scattered soldiers to regroup on the battlefield. There was also a drumbeat that meant "retreat."

Between battles, drummer boys also helped set up camp, cook, and tend the wounded. The boys did have a little time for play. They kept their special toys, books, and even small animals in their drums.

The Civil War was the last time that drummer boys were used. Weapons became louder and more powerful. It became difficult for soldiers to hear orders from drumbeats. But acts of heroism by drummer boys were told for generations after the Civil War.

THE DRUMMER BOY

fold back

glue

JOHNNY CLEM
A TRUE STORY

Johnny Clem was born in Newark, Ohio, on August 13, 1851. He ran away from home in May 1861 to join the Union army. However, the army did not want him because he was only 9 years old. Johnny was determined, however, and finally found a regiment that would allow him to perform camp duties and act as a drummer boy even though he was not officially enlisted. Officers in the regiment donated money so that Johnny could receive a small salary, $13 a month. His fellow soldiers were said to have provided him with a shortened rifle and a small uniform.

In May 1863, at the age of 11, Johnny was permitted to officially enlist in his regiment and received normal pay. In September of that year, many members of Johnny's regiment were captured by Confederate soldiers in Georgia at the Battle of Chickamauga, but Johnny escaped by shooting the man who tried to capture him. Johnny's bravery earned him the nickname "the drummer boy of Chickamauga." He was promoted to lance corporal.

Johnny served in the Union army until the end of the war. Several years after the war had ended, he rejoined as a lieutenant. He served in the army until 1916, when he retired as a general.

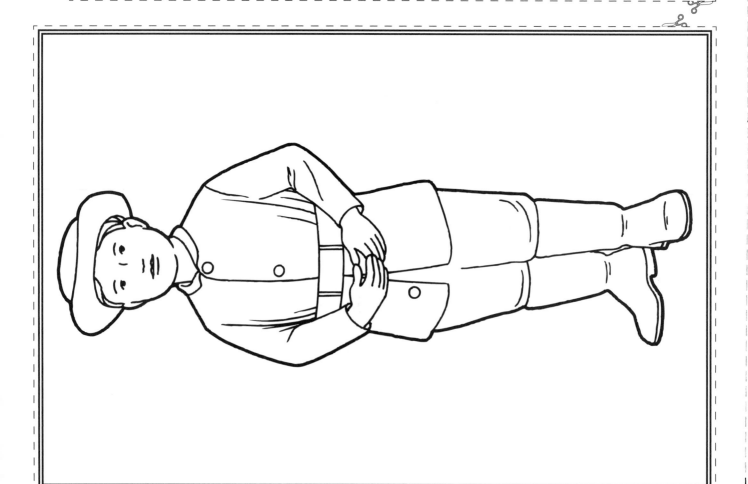

LETTERS HOME

A Civil War soldier's favorite part of the day was mail call. Between battles, camp life was dull and boring, and many soldiers were very homesick. Letters were the only way for soldiers to stay in touch with family and friends back home. Soldiers loved getting letters from home. It was one of their few forms of entertainment. They read, reread, and treasured their letters.

Students read a made-up letter to a Confederate soldier. They answer the letter by writing between the lines, just as a Civil War soldier might have done because paper was in such short supply.

STEPS TO FOLLOW

1. As a class, read "Letters from Home" on page 63 to provide background for the activity.

2. Then have students read the letter on page 62. If desired, provide background on the Battle of Chickamauga or have students do their own research. Discuss what type of news this soldier might want to share with his family at home. Students compose their own answers to the letter, writing between the lines of the letter itself.

3. Next, students color and cut out the envelope. The top and bottom stripes on the flag are red; the field is blue. Then students fold and glue as directed. They address the envelope, making sure that the address they make up is in one of the 11 Confederate states.

4. Students fold the letter and store it in the envelope.

MATERIALS

- pages 62 and 63, reproduced for each student
- crayons, colored pencils, or marking pens
- scissors
- glue
- pen or pencil

November 10, 1863

Dear Tom,

What a relief it was to get your last letter and to know that you are safe. Hurray for you and the rest of our boys for routing Rosecrans at Chickamauga! I feel certain that many more Confederate victories are to come.

We are fortunate that there has been no military activity in these parts. There are disturbing reports from elsewhere of crops being destroyed and animals being taken to feed the soldiers. Although there are no luxuries to be had these days, at least our stomachs are full. For that we are thankful.

As always I remain your loving sister,

Anne

Letters from Home

Soldiers wrote many letters. At the beginning of the war, they had to spend their own money on paper, pens, and stamps. Later, women's groups in the North raised money to provide Union troops with writing materials. The post office allowed Union soldiers to send letters for free.

Confederate soldiers weren't so lucky. At the start of the war, the South did not have a postal service. Eventually one was founded, but it never worked very well. Confederate soldiers also lacked writing supplies. Many troops made their own ink from berries and used goose quills or cornstalks as pens. They wrote their replies on the letters they received, writing between the lines of the old letters.

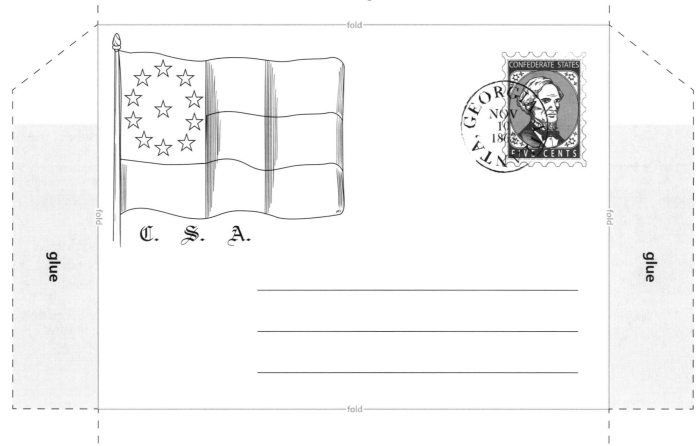

fold

fold

fold

fold

glue

glue

C. S. A.

CONFEDERATE STATES
FIVE CENTS

CIVIL WAR RECIPES

Both armies provided small meals called rations for their soldiers. Union soldiers had salted meat, biscuits (called hardtack), and coffee. Confederate soldiers had bacon, cornbread (called johnnycake), and tea. On both sides, supply trains were often delayed, so soldiers were left to fend for themselves. They hunted small animals, picked berries, and took vegetables from nearby gardens.

Students assemble their own cookbook of Civil War recipes from the battlefield.

MATERIALS

- pages 65–68, reproduced for each student
- colored pencils or fine-tip markers
- scissors
- hole punch
- 18" (46 cm) pieces of ribbon or yarn

STEPS TO FOLLOW

1. Have students color and cut out the recipe pages. Fold each page first on the horizontal fold line, then on the vertical fold line.

2. Direct students to punch holes as indicated on each sheet.

3. Instruct students to assemble the pages, one inside of the other, making sure page numbers are sequential.

4. Direct students to thread a strip of ribbon or yarn through the punched holes and secure with a knot and a bow to create the recipe book.

5. Have students read the recipes to each other and discuss which ones they would have eaten if they had been Civil War soldiers.

   Note: Since the recipes do not have exact measurements and several involve the cooking of wild animals, remind students *not* to try any of the recipes at home.

RECIPES

CIVIL WAR

Both armies provided small meals called rations for their soldiers. Union soldiers had salted meat, crackers (called hardtack), and coffee. Confederate soldiers had bacon, cornbread (called johnnycake), and tea. On both sides, long distances and bad weather often delayed supply trains. By the time food finally arrived, soldiers discovered it was stale, rotten, or full of bugs. Many times, soldiers were left to fend for themselves. They hunted small animals, picked berries, and took vegetables from nearby gardens. Some Civil War soldiers became excellent cooks, even though they had only simple ingredients and cooked in a skillet over a campfire.

TABLE OF CONTENTS

Swamp Cabbage Stew
(Confederate recipe)

Ingredients
- salt pork
- cabbage
- tomatoes
- onion
- garlic
- cayenne pepper

Directions
1. Fry chunks of pork in a skillet over campfire.
2. Slice the vegetables and add them to the skillet.
3. Add spices. Cayenne pepper is hot, so add just a little unless the soldiers like it really spicy.
4. Cook slowly for four hours.

①

Johnnycake
(Confederate recipe)

Ingredients
- 2 cups cornmeal
- ⅔ cup milk
- 2 t. baking soda
- ½ t. salt
- 2 T. lard
- butter or molasses

Directions
1. Mix cornmeal, milk, baking soda, and salt. Beat until you have a stiff batter.
2. Melt lard in skillet.
3. Spoon the batter into melted lard.
4. Fry over low flame until brown.
5. When cool, spread cornbread with butter or molasses.

⑫

fold 2

fold 1

Fried Squirrel
(Union and Confederate recipe)

Ingredients
- 1 squirrel
- 1 cup flour
- ¼ cup lard

Directions
1. Skin and clean squirrel.
2. Cut into pieces like a chicken.
3. Rolls pieces in flour.
4. Fry in a skillet until brown.

②

Fried Hardtack
(Union recipe)

Ingredients
- 3 or 4 hardtack
- water
- bacon grease

Directions
1. Soak hardtack in water to soften.
2. Add bacon grease to skillet. Heat.
3. Add softened hardtack and fry until toasted.

⑪

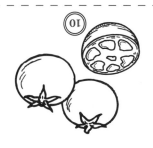

(3)

Browned Tomatoes

(Confederate recipe)

Ingredients

lard

4 to 8 tomatoes

flour

salt and pepper

Directions

1. Melt lard in skillet.
2. Cut tomatoes in half, roll them in flour, and place them faceup in skillet.
3. Sprinkle with salt and pepper.
4. Turn over and brown thoroughly.

(10)

Pickled Pigs Feet

(Union and Confederate recipe)

Ingredients

4 pigs feet

water

vinegar

salt and pepper

Directions

1. Place pigs feet in pan. Add water.
2. Boil pigs feet until tender.
3. Pack them in a jar and add vinegar to cover.
4. Add salt and pepper to taste.

fold 2

fold 1

Spit-Roasted Rabbit

(Union and Confederate recipe)

Ingredients

1 rabbit

salt and pepper

Directions

1. Skin and clean rabbit.
2. Tie front and back paws on a spit with twine.
3. Roast over open fire, turning often.
4. Season with salt and pepper.

(4)

Bean Soup

(Union recipe)

Ingredients

½ pound uncooked navy beans

water

ham shank

1 cup diced uncooked potatoes

2 chopped tomatoes

salt and pepper

Directions

1. Cover beans with cold water. Soak overnight.
2. The next morning, cook beans in water until tender. Strain.
3. Cover ham with cold water. Cook slowly until tender, skimming off fat regularly.
4. Add beans and potatoes to pot. Simmer.
5. Add tomatoes, salt, and pepper. Simmer.

(9)

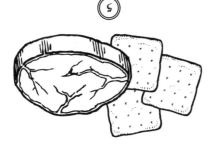

"Skillygalee"
(Union recipe)

Ingredients
lard
salted pork
3 hardtack (crackers)

Directions
1. Melt lard in skillet.
2. Add salted pork. Fry.
3. Crumble hardtack into small pieces. (Soak in coffee or water a minute if they are too hard to crumble.)
4. Add hardtack to pork and mix.

Scrap Stock
(Union recipe)

Ingredients
8 to 10 cups of vegetable and fruit scraps (carrot tops, onion peels, ends of squash and pumpkins, apple cores, etc.)
water
chopped garlic
salt

Directions
1. Put all ingredients in pot and bring to a boil.
2. Reduce heat to simmer.
3. Strain, or throw out vegetable/fruit scraps.
4. Drink broth, or save it as stock to use in cooking other things later.

fold 2

fold 1

"Coosh"
(Confederate recipe)

Ingredients
bacon
cornmeal
water

Directions
1. Fry bacon in skillet.
2. Add cornmeal and water.
3. Cook until mixture becomes a thick brown-gray similar to the consistency of oatmeal.

Crawdads (also called crayfish)
(Confederate recipe)

Ingredients
2 to 3 dozen crawdads
juice from 1 lemon
water
chopped onion and garlic
chopped celery with leaves

Directions
1. Gather crawdads from nearby stream. Chop off tails. Save tails. Give rest to camp dogs.
2. In pot, boil lemon, water, onion, garlic, and celery.
3. Add crawdad tails and boil again.
4. Reduce heat and cook until meat is white.
5. Eat hot, or put in cold water to eat later.

WHAT'S A PUP TENT?

In the Union army, tent camps were set up during the mild months of the year. A two-man tent was called a pup tent. Men joked that only a dog could crawl under it and stay dry.

Students create their own model of a pup tent. They discuss and write about what life must have been like for the soldiers living in these conditions.

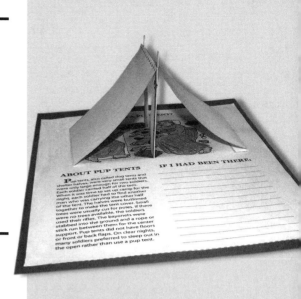

STEPS TO FOLLOW

1. As a class, read the information about pup tents on page 70. Then have students write a paragraph about how they would have coped with such conditions.

2. Have students color the patterns on pages 70 and 71.

3. Direct students to assemble the project as follows:
   a. Cut out the patterns.
   b. Glue page 70 onto the construction paper.
   c. Fold the tent on the fold lines and glue to page 70.
   d. Cut marked slits on each side of the tent and the folded rifles.
   e. Slip the folded rifles into the slits to create the supports for the tent.

4. Students fold the tent down for storage in the pocket.

MATERIALS

- pages 70 and 71, reproduced for each student
- 9" x 12" (23 x 30.5 cm) colored construction paper
- crayons, colored pencils, or marking pens
- scissors
- glue
- pencil or pen

WHAT'S A PUP TENT?

glue

ABOUT PUP TENTS

Pup tents, also called dog tents and shelter halves, were very small tents that were only large enough for two soldiers. Each soldier carried half of the tent. When it was time to set up camp for the night, each soldier had to find another man who was carrying the other half of the tent. The halves were buttoned together to make the tent cover. Small trees were usually cut for poles. If there were no trees available, the soldiers used their rifles. The bayonets were stabbed into the ground and a rope or stick run between them for the center support. Pup tents did not have floors or front or back flaps. On clear nights, many soldiers preferred to sleep out in the open rather than use a pup tent.

IF I HAD BEEN THERE:

_____
_____
_____
_____
_____
_____
_____
_____
_____
_____
_____

Pup Tent and Rifle Patterns

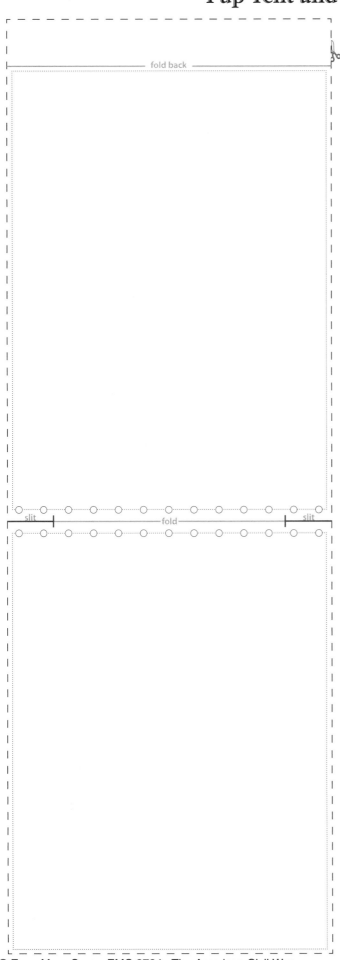

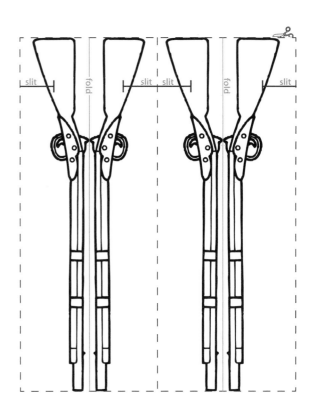

Pocket 6

WOMEN DURING THE WAR

FAST FACTS

See page 2 for instructions on how to prepare the Fast Facts bookmark and pocket label. As you complete the activities in this pocket, read the Fast Facts bookmark frequently for a quick review.

ABOUT

Reproduce this page for students. Read and discuss the information, incorporating available library and multimedia resources. Refer to this information page as you complete the activities in this pocket.

ACTIVITIES

Students read to learn about the important contributions of Clara Barton. They write and answer questions about this great woman.

By the end of the war, American women had sewn hundreds of thousands of quilts for soldiers on both sides of the war. Students make their own quilt square.

Students read the fictional diary of a young Confederate girl, and then re-create her diary by constructing a booklet.

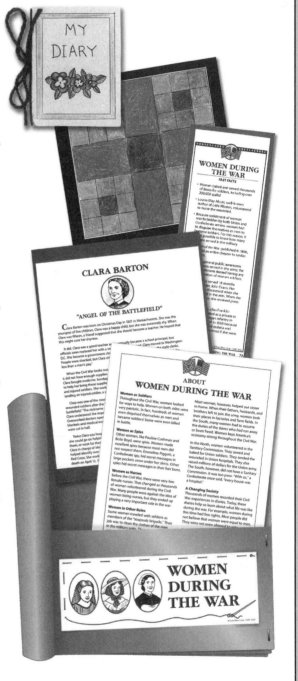

WOMEN DURING THE WAR

WOMEN DURING THE WAR

FAST FACTS

- Women baked and sewed thousands of items for soldiers, including over 200,000 quilts!

- Louisa May Alcott, well-known author of *Little Women*, volunteered to nurse the wounded.

- Because enlistment of women was forbidden by both Union and Confederate armies, women had to disguise themselves as men to become soldiers. For this reason, it is not possible to know how many women served in the military.

- *Women of the War,* published in 1866, devoted an entire chapter to soldier heroines.

- Despite general public awareness that women served in the army, the War Department denied having any documentation of women soldiers.

- Mary Owens served 18 months under the alias John Evans. Her identity was discovered when she was wounded in the arm. When she returned home, she received press coverage.

- Sarah Edmonds, alias Franklin Thompson, enlisted as a private in the Second Michigan Infantry in 1861. She deserted in 1863 because she had contracted malaria and feared being discovered if she were hospitalized.

ABOUT
WOMEN DURING THE WAR

Women as Soldiers

Throughout the Civil War, women looked for ways to help. Women on both sides were very patriotic. In fact, hundreds of women even disguised themselves as men and became soldiers! Some were even killed in battle.

Women as Spies

Other women, like Pauline Cushman and Belle Boyd, were spies. Women made excellent spies because most men did not suspect them. Emmeline Piggott, a Confederate spy, hid secret messages in large pockets sewn under her skirts. Other spies hid secret messages in their hair buns.

Women as Nurses

Before the Civil War, there were very few female nurses. That changed as thousands of women volunteered during the Civil War. Many people were against the idea of women being nurses, but they ended up playing a very important role in the war.

Women in Other Roles

Some women traveled with soldiers as members of the "soapsuds brigade." Their job was to clean the clothes of the men in the military units. These brave women risked their lives, even though many men would have preferred that they had played their part off the battlefield.

Most women, however, helped out closer to home. When their fathers, husbands, and brothers left to join the army, women took their places in factories and farm fields. In the South, many women had to assume the duties of the slaves who had run away or been freed. Women kept America's economy strong throughout the Civil War.

In the North, women volunteered in the Sanitary Commission. They sewed and baked for Union soldiers. They tended the wounded in Union hospitals. They also raised millions of dollars for the Union army. The South, however, did not have a Sanitary Commission. It was too poor. "With us," a Confederate once said, "every house was a hospital."

A Changing Society

Thousands of women recorded their Civil War experiences in diaries. Today, these diaries help us learn about what life was like during the war. For example, women during this time had few rights. Most people did not believe that women were equal to men. They were not even allowed to vote.

However, the work that women did during the war impressed many people across the country. It changed the way men thought of women. It also changed the way women thought of themselves.

    The American Civil War • EMC 3724 • © Evan-Moor Corp.

CLARA BARTON: "ANGEL OF THE BATTLEFIELD"

There were many heroines on both sides of the war. The name Clara Barton stands out as one of the most famous. She took medical supplies to some of the worst battle sites and worked tirelessly as a nurse. A doctor on the battlefield said, "If heaven ever sent out a holy angel, she must be one."

After students read a biography of Clara Barton, they write and answer questions about her.

STEPS TO FOLLOW

1. As a class, read the biography of Clara Barton on page 76. Refer to the "About" page for additional information. Discuss Barton's contributions during and after the war.

2. Direct students to write four questions on the biography of Clara Barton. They should write one question that starts with each of these words: *what, where, why, how*. Then they write the paragraph and sentence number where the answer can be found.

3. Have students join up with a partner and take turns reading questions for the partner to answer.

4. Then direct students to glue the biography to the front of the construction paper and the questions and answers they wrote to the back of the paper.

MATERIALS

- page 76, reproduced for each student
- writing paper
- 9" x 12" (23 x 30.5 cm) colored construction paper
- pencil or pen
- scissors
- glue

CLARA BARTON

"ANGEL OF THE BATTLEFIELD"

Clara Barton was born on Christmas Day in 1821 in Massachusetts. She was the youngest of five children. Clara was a happy child, but she was extremely shy. When Clara was fifteen, a friend suggested that she should become a teacher. He hoped that this might cure her shyness.

It did. Clara was a good teacher and eventually became a school principal, but officials soon replaced her with a man. Sad and frustrated, Clara moved to Washington, D.C. She became a government clerk and earned the same salary as the male clerks. People were shocked, but Clara simply responded, "I shall never do a man's work for less than a man's pay."

When the Civil War broke out, the Union was unprepared for so many casualties. It did not have enough supplies to treat its wounded soldiers. With her own money, Clara bought medicine, bandages, and food. Then she organized a group of women to help her bring these supplies to battlefield hospitals. Clara stayed and cared for sick and injured soldiers. She worked in the bloodiest battlefields of the war. Once, while tending an injured soldier, a stray bullet whizzed through her sleeve and killed the man.

Clara was one of the most admired women of the Civil War. When caring for wounded soldiers after the Battle of Antietam, a doctor called her the "angel of the battlefield." The nickname stuck for the rest of her life. Unlike many people at the time, Clara understood the importance of cleanliness. Army hospitals were filled with disease. Overworked doctors operated with bloodstained coats and dirty tools. Clara washed blankets and medical instruments. She cleaned wounds with fresh water. Disease rates were cut in half.

Twice Clara was hospitalized for sickness and exhaustion. When people asked how she could go on helping the soldiers, Clara asked back, "What could I do but go with them, or work for them and my country?" At the end of the war, President Lincoln put Clara in charge of identifying missing Union soldiers who had been killed. Her records helped identify over one thousand dead soldiers. In 1881, Clara founded the American Red Cross. She worked hard helping victims of wars and natural disasters until her death on April 12, 1912.

   The American Civil War • EMC 3724 • © Evan-Moor Corp.

QUILTING FOR A CAUSE

Women made hundreds of thousands of quilts for soldiers during the Civil War. There were many different patterns and sizes, and women took great pride in their handiwork.

Students read the information about quilting, then create and decorate their own quilt square.

STEPS TO FOLLOW

1. With the class, read and discuss "Quilting for a Cause" on page 78.

2. Have students color and cut out the quilt square on page 79.

3. Direct students to glue their quilt square to construction paper.

4. Before students store their quilt square in Pocket 6, you may wish to arrange them on a classroom wall to form a complete Civil War quilt.

MATERIALS

- pages 78 and 79, reproduced for each student
- 9" x 9" (23 cm) black construction paper
- crayons, colored pencils, or markers
- scissors
- glue

QUILTING FOR A CAUSE

Throughout the Civil War, women on both sides were eager to help their soldiers. Both Union and Confederate armies needed warm quilts for their troops. They specifically asked for quilts that measured seven feet long by four feet wide. This was the best size for army cots.

Northern women were excellent quilt makers. They lived where winters were cold and people used more blankets. Quilts could be made using small scraps of material they already had at home. Pieces of old blankets, shirts, and even uniforms were used in the quilts. Before the war, Northern women had experience sewing quilts for charities and church organizations or to be raffled off at county fairs. In the years leading up to the war, antislavery fairs were held throughout Northern states. Many quilts at these fairs had words and drawings that described the wrongs of slavery.

Southern women did not quilt as much as Northern women. The weather was warmer, and many women had slaves who did most of the sewing. But these women worked hard to improve their sewing skills, and even organized parties called quilting bees. By the end of the war, fabric in the South was scarce. Women tore up mattresses and carpets, bound the edges, and sent them to the troops. When Union soldiers captured a Confederate town, one of the first things they did was look for food and quilts. Southern women learned to hide them both.

Today there are not many quilts left from the Civil War. Many were worn out from so much use. Some soldiers were even buried with their quilt. The few quilts that have survived are in museums throughout the United States.

 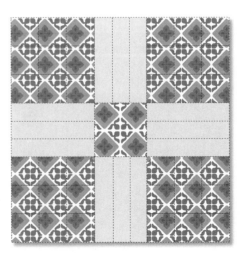

NINE-PATCH QUILT SQUARES

   The American Civil War • EMC 3724 • © Evan-Moor Corp.

NINE-PATCH QUILT SQUARE

Color the nine-patch quilt square.

Cut on the dotted lines.

Glue the quilt square to a piece of construction paper.

MATERIALS

- pages 81–83, reproduced for each student
- 5" x 8" (13 x 20 cm) colored construction paper
- fine-tip markers or colored pencils
- scissors
- stapler
- 18" (46 cm) yarn or ribbon

VIRGINIA MATTHEWS: DIARY OF A YOUNG GIRL

The Civil War changed the lives of all Americans, but especially those living in the South. Virginia Matthews is a fictional girl whose experiences represent those of many children during the war. Her diary chronicles the hardships and struggles that Southerners faced throughout the war.

Students re-create Virginia's diary by assembling a booklet. They draw pictures to illustrate specific passages.

STEPS TO FOLLOW

1. Instruct students to cut out Virginia's diary on pages 81–83 and fold each page first on the horizontal fold line, and then on the verticle fold line.

2. Have students fold the construction paper in half and then open it. Arrange the diary pages in chronological order, matching fold lines, and center them inside the construction paper cover.

3. Help students staple the diary on the inside fold.

4. Have students place a piece of yarn or ribbon in the inside fold, then flip the book over and tie a bow on the outside of the cover.

5. Direct students to decorate the cover and draw pictures that illustrate specific passages from the diary.

6. Then have students read the diary as a class, in small groups, or independently.

Virginia Matthews: Diary of a Young Girl

"Sherman's army is scattered across Atlanta....my father fears for our safety and will not permit us to leave his sight."

—Virginia Matthews

Virginia Matthews is a fictional girl whose experiences represent those of many Southerners during the Civil War. The diary entries show many of the hardships endured by Southerners. Families that were wealthy and owned many slaves when the war started found themselves poor and hungry after the war ended. They were not used to working hard and had to learn to rely on themselves. Like most Southerners, Virginia supported the war and wanted the Confederacy to win. But by the time this fictional diary begins, the South had lost many important battles, and it was obvious that life would never be the same again.

December 15, 1864

About three miles from home, we saw what they call the "Burnt Country." The Union army has burned every bale of cotton they could find and has destroyed everything in sight. There was not even a chicken left to eat.

①

August 9, 1865

I do not believe life will ever again be as fine as before the Union army invaded. I thank heaven I was born a Southerner and not a horrible Yankee.

⑩

⟨2⟩

January 10, 1865

I used to think I was very brave, but now that I have seen the destruction the Yankees have caused, I am very afraid.

⟨6⟩

August 2, 1865

Mary showed me some very pretty dresses in the shop window yesterday. Perhaps one day I will be able to have such things again.

fold 2

fold 1

February 13, 1865

Father gave me a beautiful red ribbon to trim my dress with. It is such a pleasure to have something nice after so much hardship.

⟨3⟩

July 23, 1865

Mrs. Smith had all of us for supper yesterday, and it was quite grand to dine in the old style. This morning, though, I had to rise early to help Mother clean the house. I am very tired from the effort.

⟨8⟩

April 26, 1865

We have gone to live with Aunt Elizabeth and Uncle Charles. We have very little meat and only a few vegetables, though I am getting used to such hardships.

March 19, 1865

We haven't had milk for a week now. Father traded our milk cow for some chickens and barrels of flour and corn. What will we do when those supplies are gone?

March 30, 1865

We shall have to leave our home. Mother says she doesn't know if we will ever be able to come back. I went to the slave quarters tonight to say goodbye and then went to bed crying.

April 6, 1865

The fighting is coming closer and closer. We do not know what our future holds. I am very afraid to consider what might happen.

*The South surrendered three days later.

5

6

Pocket 7

WAR TECHNOLOGY

FAST FACTS

See page 2 for instructions on how to prepare
the Fast Facts bookmark and pocket label. As
you complete the activities in this pocket, read
the Fast Facts bookmark frequently for a quick
review.

ABOUT

Reproduce this page for students. Read and
discuss the information, incorporating available
library and multimedia resources. Refer to this
information page as you complete the activities
in this pocket.

ACTIVITIES

Students learn Morse Code and decode one of
General Grant's messages to President Lincoln.

Before the Civil War, ships were made from wood.
Students learn about the invention of ironclad
ships as they create a booklet about the USS
Monitor and the CSS *Virginia*.

The Civil War was the first war where photography
was widely used. Students read about how
photographs were made during the Civil War
and compare those methods to the ones used
today.

WAR TECHNOLOGY

WAR TECHNOLOGY

FAST FACTS

- The Civil War was the first time people communicated by telegraph, transported troops by trains, and used ironclad warships and submarines in naval combat.

- The Confederate submarine named *H.L. Hunley* was the first submersible to engage and sink a warship. In 1995, the 40-foot submarine was discovered at the bottom of the Atlantic Ocean off Sullivan's Island, South Carolina.

- The "Gatling Gun" was a crank-operated weapon with 6 barrels. It was one of the first machine guns used for war.

- Ambulances were used for the first time during the Civil War. In both the Union and Confederate armies, cooks and musicians worked as stretcher bearers, transporting the wounded in four-wheeled horse-drawn carriages.

- Samuel F.B. Morse's first telegraph, produced in 1846, could only send a signal 40 feet (12 meters). But by the mid-1850s, Morse and his business partners had established a national telegraph network.

- When the Civil War began, well-known photographer Mathew Brady's eyesight was too poor to operate a camera himself. He hired about 300 cameramen, who took thousands of photographs of all aspects of the war.

ABOUT
WAR TECHNOLOGY

The First Modern War

The Civil War has been called the first modern war. Many devices that are common today were first used in the Civil War. Other technology, like submarines and the telegraph, were invented earlier. But it was the war that made them popular.

On the Battlefield

Some inventions were created for the battlefield. A machine gun called the Gatling Gun was first used in the Civil War. People were shocked at the huge number of deaths it produced. Land mines also caused a lot of destruction. Confederate soldiers buried shells a few inches below ground that exploded on contact.

At Sea

New technology was also used during battles at sea. Underwater mines were first used on a wide scale by Confederate forces to protect key waterways. Mines damaged over twenty Union ships and destroyed many others. The mere suspicion that mines were present would force the cancellation of Union naval operations.

Ironclad ships replaced wooden ships. The Confederates built the first one from the burned hull of the USS *Merrimack*. The new ironclad was renamed the CSS *Virginia*. The first battle using ironclads was between the CSS *Virginia* and the USS *Monitor*.

In the Skies

Hot-air balloons were first used by the Union army during the Civil War. In 1862, during the Warwick-Yorktown Siege, Union General George McClellan used two gas balloons called the Intrepid and the Constitution. They were launched almost daily to observe Confederate defenses. Confederate forces responded with their own use of surveillance balloons.

Photography

The Civil War was the first war to be widely photographed. Photographers took pictures of slaves, battles, and camp life. It was the first time many soldiers had ever had their photo taken. Americans were fascinated with these pictures. They were so different from the lifeless paintings everyone was used to. When photos of dead soldiers from the Battle of Antietam were published in newspapers, people were horrified. It was the first time photos of war casualties had been made available to the public. Photography even changed the way some people looked at slavery. Photographs of slaves, with their tired faces and shabby clothes, convinced Northerners more than ever that slavery had to end.

Ultimately, advances in technology changed the way people waged war.

THE TELEGRAPH AND MORSE CODE

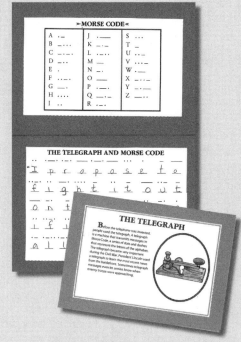

As the Civil War progressed, mobile telegraph stations and hastily strung wires began to connect scattered military units. Union generals McClellan and Grant sent frequent dispatches to the War Department telegraph office, where President Lincoln received news from the front.

Students learn Morse Code and decode one of General Grant's messages to President Lincoln.

STEPS TO FOLLOW

1. As a class, read the information about the telegraph on page 88. Then have students study the Morse Code alphabet. Note that only letters have been included.

2. Instruct students to fold the construction paper in half.

3. Direct students to cut out "The Telegraph" box and glue it to the front of the paper folder.

4. Students then cut out the Morse Code alphabet and glue it to the top inside portion of the folder.

5. Instruct students to cut out General Grant's message and glue it to the bottom inside portion of the folder.

6. Have students decode General Grant's message, writing the letters on the lines below the code.

   Answer: *I propose to fight it out on this line if it takes all summer.*

7. Have students make up messages of their own, then have partners decode the messages using the form on page 89. Have students glue their messages on the back of the folder.

MATERIALS

- pages 88 and 89, reproduced for each student
- 9" x 12" (23 x 30.5 cm) colored construction paper
- scissors
- pencil
- glue

THE TELEGRAPH AND MORSE CODE

❧·MORSE CODE·❧

A	._	J	.___	S	...		
B	_...	K	_._	T	_		
C	_._.	L	._..	U	.._		
D	_..	M	__	V	..._		
E	.	N	_.	W	.__		
F	.._.	O	___	X	_.._		
G	__.	P	.__.	Y	_.__		
H	....	Q	__._	Z	__..		
I	..	R	._.				

THE TELEGRAPH

Before the telephone was invented, people used the telegraph. A telegraph is a machine that transmits messages in Morse Code, a series of dots and dashes that represent the letters of the alphabet. The telegraph became very important during the Civil War. President Lincoln used a telegraph to learn the most recent news from the battlefront. Sometimes telegraph messages even let armies know when enemy troops were approaching.

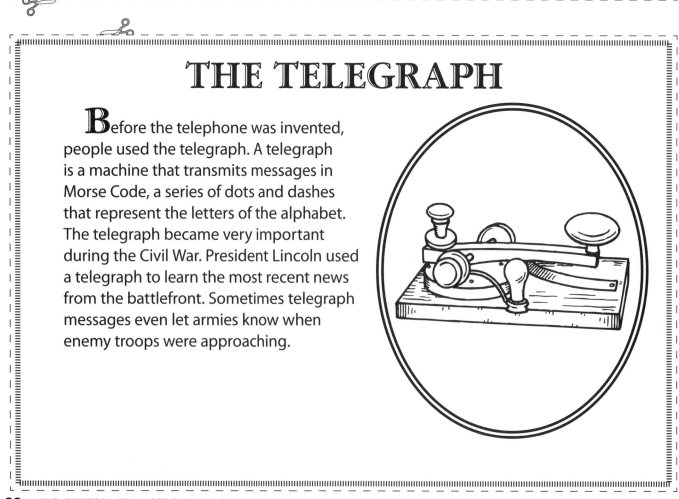

The American Civil War • EMC 3724 • © Evan-Moor Corp.

THE TELEGRAPH AND MORSE CODE

..   — .— . — .— . — .— .   ... . — . — — — —

"
— —— — —— — —— — —— — —— — —— — —— — ——

..— .. —. — . . — . — .. —. — —. — .— . — . — — — —

— — —. —. — ... .— — .. — . .
— — —— — —— — —— — —— — —— — —— — —— — ——

.. ... .—. .. — — .—. —.. . ...
— — —— — —— — —— — —— — —— — —— — —— — ——

. — .. —. — . .. .— — .— — . .—.
"
— — —— — —— — —— — —— — —— — —— —.

General Ulysses S. Grant
Battle of the Wilderness

MY CODED MESSAGE

Code:

Code:

Code:

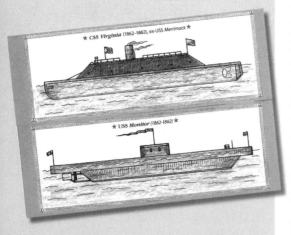

IRONCLADS

Before the Civil War, battleships were made from wood. During the Civil War, however, ships called ironclads were made by armoring ships with thick iron plates. Ironclads changed the way enemies fought one another. The first battle of ironclads was on March 9, 1862, between the USS *Monitor* and the CSS *Virginia*. Both sides claimed victory. The *Monitor* stopped the Confederate ironclad from destroying the Federal fleet, but the *Virginia* blocked the James River and closed this approach to Richmond to Union use.

Students create a booklet about the USS *Monitor* and the CSS *Virginia*.

MATERIALS

- pages 91 and 92, reproduced for each student
- 9" x 12" (23 x 30.5 cm) blue construction paper
- scissors
- pencil
- colored pencils
- glue

STEPS TO FOLLOW

1. Have students read the information about ironclads on page 92.

2. Then instruct students to fold the construction paper as shown, color and cut out the ironclad illustrations on page 91, and glue them to the outside flaps of the paper.

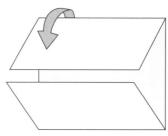

3. Instruct students to cut out the information about the ironclads on page 92 and glue it to the center inside section of the paper.

4. Then have students cut out the writing form on page 92 and write about why this new weapon was so important. Students then glue the form to the bottom inside section of the paper.

The American Civil War • EMC 3724 • © Evan-Moor Corp.

IRONCLADS

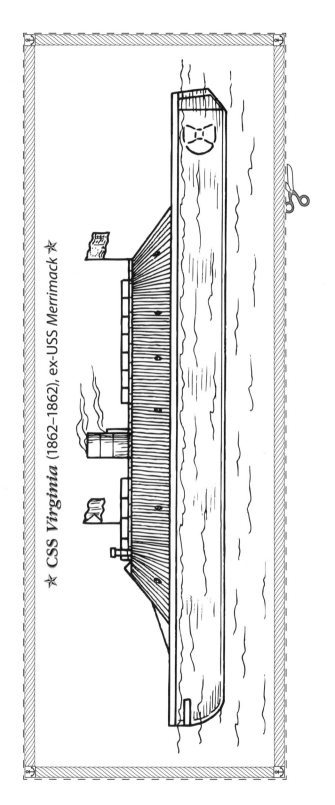

★ *CSS Virginia* (1862–1862), ex-USS *Merrimack* ★

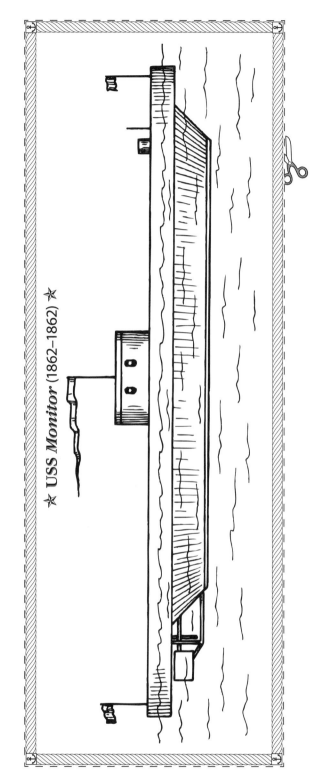

★ *USS Monitor* (1862–1862) ★

IRONCLADS

One of history's most important weapons was invented during the Civil War. It was called the ironclad. Unlike a wooden ship, a cannonball simply bounced off an ironclad. The Confederates were the first to begin work on this secret weapon. They quietly raised a sunken Union ship called the *Merrimack*, covered it with sheets of iron, and renamed it the *Virginia*. Rumors of the project caught Northerners by surprise. The Union scrambled to build an ironclad. They built the *Monitor*, and on March 9, 1862, the two ironclads met in battle. The ships fought so closely that they actually collided. After many hours, the battle ended in a tie. What was certain, however, was that the ironclads were the ships of the future.

Why was this weapon so important?

_____

_____

_____

_____

_____

The American Civil War • EMC 3724 • © Evan-Moor Corp.

PHOTOGRAPHY— THEN AND NOW

The Civil War was the first war where photography was widely used.

Students read about how photographs were made during the Civil War and compare those methods to the ones used today.

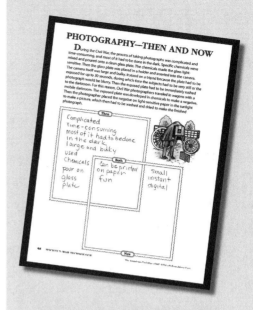

STEPS TO FOLLOW

1. As a class, read the information on page 94 about the photography process used during the Civil War.

2. Then instruct students to complete the Venn diagram comparing photographic methods then and now. This may be done as a class or independently.

MATERIALS

- page 94, reproduced for each student
- pencil

PHOTOGRAPHY—THEN AND NOW

During the Civil War, the process of taking photographs was complicated and time-consuming, and most of it had to be done in the dark. Specific chemicals were mixed and poured onto a clean glass plate. The chemicals made the glass light-sensitive. Then the glass plate was placed in a holder and inserted into the camera. The camera itself was large and bulky. It stood on a tripod because the plate had to be exposed for up to 30 seconds, during which time the subjects had to be very still or the photograph would be blurry. Then the exposed plate had to be immediately rushed to the darkroom. For this reason, Civil War photographers traveled in wagons with a mobile darkroom. The exposed plate was developed in chemicals to make a negative. Then the photographer placed the negative on light-sensitive paper in the sunlight to make a picture, which then had to be washed and dried to make the finished photograph.

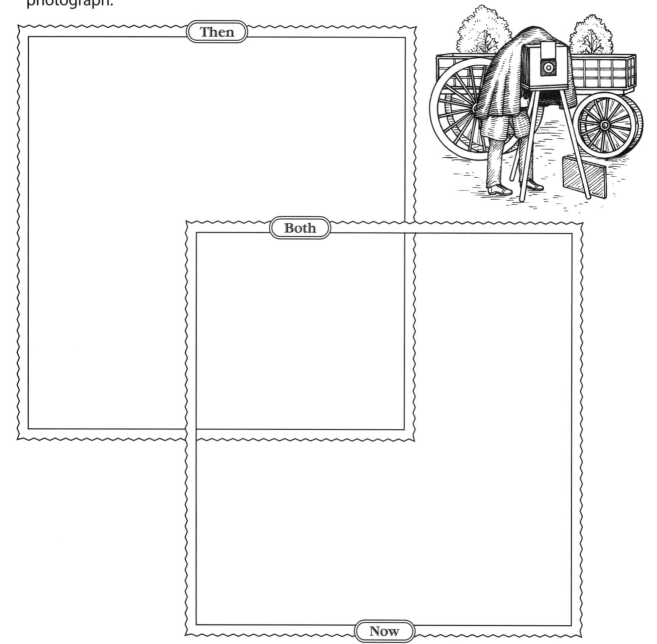

Then

Both

Now

Name _____   Date _____

CIVIL WAR REFLECTION SHEET

Directions: Please fill out this sheet after you have completed your book.

1. When I look through my Civil War book, I feel _____

   because _____

2. The project I enjoyed the most was the _____

   because _____

3. The project I enjoyed the least was the _____

   because _____

4. Three things I am most proud of in my Civil War book are _____

   _____

   _____

   _____

5. Three things I would do differently to improve my Civil War book are _____

   _____

   _____

   _____

6. Three things I learned about the Civil War that I did not know before doing this project are

   _____

   _____

   _____

   _____

7. Explain one aspect of the Civil War and tell how it has affected our lives today.

   _____

   _____

   _____

Name _____ Date _____

CIVIL WAR EVALUATION SHEET

Directions: Look through all the pockets and evaluate how well the activities were completed. Use the following point system:

6 Outstanding	5 Excellent	4 Very Good	3 Satisfactory	2 Some Effort	1 Little Effort	0 No Effort

Self-Evaluation	Peer Evaluation	Teacher Evaluation

Name: _____

___ completed assignments

___ followed directions

___ had correct information

___ edited writing

___ showed creativity

___ added color

___ **total points**

Comments _____

_____

_____

_____

_____

_____

_____

_____

_____

_____

_____

_____

Name: _____

___ completed assignments

___ followed directions

___ had correct information

___ edited writing

___ showed creativity

___ added color

___ **total points**

Comments _____

_____

_____

_____

_____

_____

_____

_____

_____

_____

_____

_____

___ completed assignments

___ followed directions

___ had correct information

___ edited writing

___ showed creativity

___ added color

___ **total points**

___ **grade**

Comments _____

_____

_____

_____

_____

_____

_____

_____

_____

_____

_____

_____